THE UNIVERSITY OF WINCHESTER

Martial Rose Library
Tel: 01962 827306

SEVEN DAY LOAN ITEM

To be returned on or before the day marked above, subject to r

Being and Having in Shakespeare

Oxford Wells Shakespeare Lectures

Being and Having in Shakespeare

KATHARINE EISAMAN MAUS

OXFORD
UNIVERSITY PRESS

OXFORD
UNIVERSITY PRESS

Great Clarendon Street, Oxford, OX2 6DP,
United Kingdom

Oxford University Press is a department of the University of Oxford.
It furthers the University's objective of excellence in research, scholarship,
and education by publishing worldwide. Oxford is a registered trade mark of
Oxford University Press in the UK and in certain other countries

© Katharine Eisaman Maus 2013

The moral rights of the author have been asserted

First Edition published in 2013

Impression: 1

British Library Cataloguing in Publication Data
Data available

ISBN 978–0–19–969800–4

Printed in Great Britain by
Clays Ltd, St Ives plc

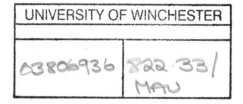

For Marianne Innis

Acknowledgments

I am profoundly grateful to Oxford University and Oxford University Press for asking me to present the Oxford Wells Shakespeare Lectures in November 2010; this book is the outcome of that invitation. I have presented excerpts as well at Stanford University, the University of Chicago, Wesleyan University, Ohio State University, Michigan State University, the 2010 Conference of the International Association of University Professors of English, the 2010 Ohio Valley Shakespeare Conference, the 2011 International Shakespeare Association Congress in Prague, and the Shakespeare Association Annual Meeting for several years running. Attentive and inquisitive audience members at all these events much improved the final product. My work benefited enormously from my inclusion in two lively and informative Folger Institute seminars on early modern conceptions of property, one led by Craig Muldrew and the other by John Pocock and Gordon Schochet. I'm also indebted to the students in my spring 2011 graduate seminar at the University of Virginia on the topic of property in Renaissance drama.

Contents

1

Being and Having in *Richard II*

"Above all, [the prince] must refrain from seizing the property of others, because men forget the death of their father more quickly than the loss of their patrimony."

Machiavelli, The Prince

In Shakespeare's *Richard II*, just before King Richard is stripped of the monarchy, the onlooking Bishop of Carlisle makes an ominous prediction. Deposing an unquestionably legitimate king, he warns, will usher in long-term calamity.

> The blood of English shall manure the ground.
> And future ages groan for this foul act.
> Peace shall go sleep with Turks and infidels,
> And in this seat of peace tumultuous wars
> Shall kin with kin and kind with kind confound.
>
> (4.1.128–32)

Some of these "tumultuous wars" had, of course, been the subject of Shakespeare's previous history plays. In writing *Richard II* he looks backward in time, as it were, to locate the source or first cause of instability, the action that triggers decades of civil strife.

At first, it seems as if this original infraction may have occurred before *Richard II* begins. The play begins *in medias res*, as Bolingbroke formally accuses Richard's deputy Mowbray of the murder of Richard's and Bolingbroke's uncle, Thomas of Woodstock, Duke of Gloucester. Over the course of Act 1, it becomes clear that Bolingbroke's accusation is a veiled threat aimed at the King himself. That Richard actually ordered Gloucester's assassination is an open secret. Yet this fact cannot be acknowledged in the ceremonious form of the appeal of treason. Legally, felony is defined as an offense against the sovereign—and is not, therefore, a crime that can be committed by the sovereign. By the third scene of the play, the legal action has fizzled out and both the plaintiff, Bolingbroke, and the defendant, Mowbray, sent into exile. Perhaps justice has not been done, but Richard is still secure on his throne.

A conversation in Act 1 scene 2 between Gloucester's widow and his brother, John of Gaunt, makes it unmistakably clear that Gloucester's murder does not suffice to trigger rebellion. In this scene the Duchess of Gloucester urges Gaunt to revenge his brother's death. Yet despite the lack of any legal recourse, and despite the Duchess's argument that Richard's violence might eventually threaten Gaunt himself, Gaunt flatly refuses to take action. In Gaunt's view only God, as Richard's legitimate superior, has the right to punish him:

> God's is the quarrel; for God's substitute,
> His deputy anointed in his sight,
> Hath caused his death; the which if wrongfully,
> Let heaven revenge, for I may never lift
> An angry arm against his minister.

(1.2.37–41)

Revolting against the king seems tantamount to revolting against God himself.

Yet by the second act of this play, this robust inhibition against armed rebellion seems to evaporate. Richard's policies of taxation and of land management, perceived as confiscatory and abusive, have infuriated his subjects. The last straw is the King's seizure of the Duchy of Lancaster upon the death of John of Gaunt. This act seems to justify Gaunt's son Bolingbroke's premature return from exile at the head of an army. Nobles and commoners flock to Bolingbroke's cause, putting in train the events that lead to Richard's deposition, Bolingbroke's accession to the throne, and the imprisoned Richard's assassination. Theft rather than murder seems to constitute the last, unbearable act of tyranny that destroys the allegiance even of previously loyal subjects.

An offense against property, in other words, not an offense against life, is the remote cause of the Wars of the Roses. That property should loom so large, in *Richard II* or elsewhere, would not have surprised Machiavelli, as the epigraph to this chapter reveals. Nor would the centrality of property surprise anyone who has been reading the Shakespeare scholarship of the past fifteen years or so, much of which has focused upon the relationship between people and their possessions. Jonathan Gil Harris remarks, "if the new historicism of the 1980s and early 1990s was preoccupied...with the fashioning of early modern subjects, a pronounced tendency in the new millennium...is to engage with objects."[1]

The recent "engagement with objects," as it has manifested itself in a plethora of books and essays,[2] has engendered several lines of argument. Often, however, these arguments are not clearly distinguished from one another. In *Subject and Object in Renaissance Culture,* a 1996 anthology that helped inaugurate this line of criticism, the editors describe the attention to objects as a remedial project. Their preface opens by claiming that some nineteenth-century Renaissance scholarship—Burckhardt in particular, in his foundational *Civilization of the Renaissance in Italy*—has described the relationship between subject and object in an unduly agonistic and detached way. We would be better advised, argue the editors of the volume, to understand that relationship as more dialectical and mutually constitutive. With this rather modest premise I have absolutely no difficulty; indeed, my book will take it as axiomatic. However, many of the same essays and books assert another, more radical contention as if it were merely a further elaboration of the first claim, although it is, in fact, quite distinct. This stronger position insists not merely that subject and object are interconnected but that objects constitute subjects: indeed that, looked at closely, "subjectivity" itself is simply a hubristic illusion. Peter Stallybrass writes that in the early modern period, "objects...swell out and give material and ideological substance to the subject," and continues with a rhetorical question: "Take the value of those objects away and what is left?"[3] The answer, he implies, is nothing at all. If so, then the critic's attention to things operates as a corrective to this malign and hubristic narcissism: in Julian Yates's words, "rewriting our history as a story not of human origins but of things."[4]

Sometimes a historical narrative is advanced to explain why the supposed rupture between subject and object occurred in the first place. In *Renaissance Clothing and the Materials of Memory*, Stallybrass and his co-author, Ann Rosalind Jones, following Marx, argue that colonial trade and industrial capitalism reconceptualize material objects into infinitely interchangeable commodities, none of them desirable for their own sake but only for what they can be exchanged for. This reconceptualization requires detachment and abstraction from specific individual items—"only if one empties out the 'objectness' of the object can one make it readily exchangeable on the market." That emptying out, according to Stallybrass and Jones, "finally lead[s] to the radically dematerialized opposition between the 'individual' and his or her 'possessions.'"[5] The workings of capital, in other words, have severed for us what was once a more comfortably intimate, patently constitutive connection between objects and subjects, things and persons, property and owners, estranging the one from the other and obscuring the way in which constellations of objects facilitate the construction of the subject. Similarly Stallybrass's colleague, Margreta de Grazia, argues for a very tight connection between people and property in *King Lear,* "having is tantamount to being, *not* having is tantamount to *non*-being…persons and things cannot be alienated from one another."[6] She argues that *King Lear* is a "period piece," that its materialistic construal of subjectivity is a distinctively premodern cultural phenomenon, and that therefore critics are wrong to focus on characterological questions, which she sees as anachronistically divorced from the material concerns raised by the play. In *Hamlet Without Hamlet*, de Grazia takes a similar position, claiming that the critical focus on Hamlet's character since the eighteenth century radically distorts the play, and that we should focus instead on the way the plot turns upon landed property and inheritance.[7]

The various significations of the word "property," or its adjective form "proper," might seem to support the materialists' strong claim. The words derive from the Latin *proprius* and Romance *propre,* in which forms they have many of the same ambiguities that they have in English, so, as the Oxford English Dictionary notes: "the chronological appearance of the various shades of meaning in English does not correspond with logical development." One meaning of "proper" is "very, identical, characteristic": an object's "proper-ties" are intrinsically part of it. Yet "proper" can also mean "adjunct to a thing," that is, not intrinsic but at least theoretically separable. Thus the eighteenth-century legal writer William Blackstone de-fines property rights as "those rights which a man may acquire in and to such *external things as are unconnected with his person*" [Black-stone's italics].[8] You know you own something, Blackstone puts it, when you can "alienate" it, sell it or give it away. But if you can alienate it, then how intrinsic can it be? Other, related words simi-larly equivocate. In early modern English, the words "endowments" and "belongings" had the same range of reference as "property": possessions but also traits, characteristics. In Marlowe's *Tamburlaine, Part 1,* the bedazzled Theridamas describes Tamburlaine as: "A Scythian shepherd, so embellishéd | With nature's pride and rich-est furniture" (1.2.155–6). The word "furniture" could refer to Tamburlaine's clothing or equipment—the armor he has recently donned, or his treasury of stolen goods, which he has spread out for Theridamas to view. But it could just as well refer to his attributes, for instance the "fiery eyes" that Theridamas proceeds to admire in the next few lines.

Yet do such polysignificant terms really mean that the early mod-erns had a radically different view of the relation between property and person than "we" do today (or did back in the nineteenth and twentieth centuries)? Do they mean that Shakespeare and his con-temporaries did not distinguish subject from object, or that they considered a person the sum of his possessions: the clothes on his back, the tapestries on his wall, the cattle in his fields? Arguing for a *connection* between property and person is not the same as arguing that they are *identical*, or that the latter may simply be reduced to the former. David Hawkes writes in a review essay of some of the mate-rialists' work: "No one would suggest that subject and object are in-dependent of each other....But it is untenable to think that this interdependence means that the terms cannot be distinguished, or that to confuse them is anything other than illogical, and, as it has generally been argued, immoral." Hawkes voices objections that are primarily ethical and political: "it is wrong to treat people as things and evil to treat objects as if they were alive."[9] Yet even apart from any principled objections, the case seems highly dubious on historical grounds. Perhaps the materialist critics exaggerate the differences between pre-industrial and postindustrial worldviews in the interests of making a striking contrast, but their narrative of a Fall into com-modification seems—like most Fall narratives—too pat to be be-lieved. Moreover, there is plenty of counterevidence. *Pace* Stallybrass and de Grazia, many post-Enlightenment, post-Industrial Revolu-tion writers comment extensively on the way property entitlements support and help constitute the person. For instance, in his famous 1897 essay "The Path of Law," Supreme Court Justice Oliver Wendell Holmes argues vigorously for the importance of strongly enforced property rights, on the grounds that:

> A thing which you have enjoyed and used as your own for a long time...takes root in your being and cannot be torn away without your resenting the act and trying to defend yourself, however you came by it. The law can ask no better justifica-tion than the deepest instincts of man.[10]

Possibly, then, the link between property and person is not an un-derstanding lost in the Industrial Revolution and suddenly rediscov-ered at the end of the twentieth century, but an insight continuously available for those who look for it, and as attractive for those who, like Holmes, write about "the deepest instincts of man" as it is to those postmodern skeptics who deprecate the entire idea of deep human instincts. As David Hawkes suggests, and as Holmes's essay demonstrates, it is possible to notice the significance of property without eliminating the subject–object distinction: that is, to accept what I am calling the materialists' weak argument, without subscrib-ing to their stronger one.

In short, just because a word or a set of words has more than one meaning does not mean that the people who use those words cannot differentiate among those meanings. That's especially true when those distinctions have been elaborated and discussed since ancient times. For instance, in several dialogues Plato divides goods into three classes: "external goods" or possessions, goods of the body, and goods of the soul; but he ranks the first two as less important than the last since, in the hands of a man without wisdom, the things normally considered good are useless or positively harmful.[11] In the *Laws* "the Athenian" argues that

Virtue and great wealth are quite incompatible, at any rate great wealth as generally understood...I'll never concede to them that the rich man can become really happy without being virtuous as well: to be extremely virtuous and exceptionally rich at the same time is absolutely out of the question. "Why?" it may be asked. "Because," we shall reply, "the profit from using just *and* unjust methods is more than twice as much as that from just methods alone, and a man who only refuses to spend his money either worthily or shamefully spends only half the sum laid out by worthwhile people who are prepared to spend on worthy purposes too. So anyone who follows the opposite policy will never become richer than the man who gets twice as much profit and makes half the expenditure....The man who spends his money for honest ends and uses only just methods to come by it, will not easily become particularly rich or particularly poor".[12]

In the *Nicomachean Ethics*, Aristotle builds upon and somewhat revises Plato's account. For Aristotle, "external goods" include not merely material possessions but such gifts of fortune as friends, physical beauty, and numerous, handsome offspring. An ample endowment of such goods is certainly desirable in Aristotle's view, for the sensible reason that "it is impossible, or not easy, to do noble acts without the proper equipment" (1.8). In *The Politics*, this insight will become the basis for Aristotle's defense of private property against the communism proposed in Plato's *Republic*: one cannot very well develop the virtue of liberality if one has nothing of one's own with which to be liberal. Yet according to Aristotle wealth, however convenient, cannot make one happy by itself, for "it is merely useful for the sake of something else" (*Nicomachean Ethics* 1.5). The Stoics disputed even this instrumental, secondary role for the gifts of fortune, demarcating, or attempting to protect, the ideally imperturbable soul from all external contingencies.

Stoic *contemptus mundi* has some affinity with the strand of Jesus' teaching that distinguishes strongly between God and Mammon, and between the beggar Lazarus, welcomed to Abraham's bosom, and the rich man roasting in hell. "Lay not up treasures for yourselves upon the earth, where the moth or canker corrupt, and where thieves dig through and steal," advises Jesus in the Sermon on the

Mount. "But lay up treasures for yourselves in Heaven, where neither the moth nor canker corrupteth, and where thieves neither dig
through, nor steal. For where your treasure is, there will your heart
be also" (Matthew 6: 19–21). The distinction between spiritual and
material goods pervades the letters of Paul and the writings of the
Fathers of the Church, most of whom were trained in Greek philosophy and influenced by Plato or the Stoics.

Arguably, the distinction needs to be made again and again precisely because it is easily forgotten or confused. "Treasure in heaven"
is different from, and preferable to, "treasure upon the earth," insofar as it is incorruptible and cannot be stolen. But in Matthew's
original Greek it is still called by the noun θησαυρούς, repeated in
the verb form θησαυρίξετε (translated into English as "lay up"): both
words that primarily refer to literal storehouses and their valuable
contents. Many of Jesus' parables—the parable of the talents, of the
vineyard, of the prodigal son, of the unrighteous steward—represent
the transactions between God and man in terms of property transfers. Yet again and again, the stories are memorable because they
feature a "twist" or surprise. A vineyard owner pays those who have
worked an hour as much as those who have worked all day. A father
favors the son who has squandered his inheritance over the son who
has spent his life in dutiful toil. A servant who scrupulously con-
serves his master's money is condemned for his lack of enterprise.
An unrighteous steward, in danger of losing his position because of
financial malfeasance, regains his master's trust by committing additional frauds. These parables draw analogies between human and
divine dealings, but at the same time their scandalous outcomes suggest, paradoxically, exactly the opposite: the way God's ways defy
quotidian conceptions of relative value, normal economic incentives,
and ordinary principles of fairness.

Once Christianity becomes a state religion, the absolute rejection
of wealth and worldly ambition becomes impossible: with establishment comes an accommodation between the things of Caesar and
the things of God. And yet the accommodation remains uneasy,
revived not merely by religious radicals who periodically agitate for
the abolition of private property altogether, but by the practical difficulty of squaring material aims with spiritual ones. For instance, in
the late middle ages the mendicant orders, whose members take

vows of poverty, nonetheless accumulate large amounts of wealth, a situation that produces a struggle between those orders and the authority of the Pope. William of Ockham and Thomas Aquinas, turning their attention to this problem, develop concepts of collective, nonfamilial ownership, and differentiate between ownership claims and use claims; their ideas eventually influence the development of the modern corporation.

Ought we, then, to emphasize the way the various significations of such words as "property," "endowments," or "furniture" tend to slide together, or the way they can be teased apart? This may seem merely a six-of-one, half-a-dozen-of-the-other question of interpretive preference. But it is hardly a matter of indifference in early modern Europe. The Reformers put an end to the selling of indulgences, the purchasing of masses, the veneration of relics, and other practices that seem to them to muddle the difference between spirit and matter, worship and property transactions. In early modern England, the fraught, sometimes violent conflicts between Catholics, Anglicans, and Puritans suggest not an innocent or blithe conflation of subjects with objects or persons with things, but a serious religious and ethical conundrum for many of Shakespeare's contemporaries.[13]

Indeed, I'd argue that the simultaneously elusive and profound significance of the terms is precisely what makes their connection imaginatively productive, because dynamically unfixed and susceptible to unexpected and perilous reversal. "For where your treasure is, there will your heart be also": Jesus' saying resembles, and perhaps is the source for, Holmes's insight that what you own "takes root in your being." But what kinds of things, exactly, ought to be treasured, and where their treasury might be located, is open to question. The strong version of the materialist claim eliminates this slipperiness and ambiguity by ignoring the radical contradiction troubling the relationship between property and person in Christian thought. The ownership of things, argues Margreta de Grazia, "holds the status quo in place by locking identity into property, the subject into the object."[14] I believe that the status quo is hardly so stable, nor subjects "locked" so securely or inevitably into objects, either in *King Lear*, the topic of de Grazia's essay, or in Shakespeare's drama in general.

Shakespeare is neither a philosopher nor a theologian, but he is capable of distinguishing between material and spiritual goods. In *The Merry Wives of Windsor*, Anne Page's well-to-do father disapproves of his daughter's nobly born but impoverished suitor Fenton; he is convinced that Fenton only desires Anne "as a property," that is, because he wants to get his hands on her marriage portion. But Fenton protests:

> Albeit I will confess thy father's wealth
> Was the first motive that I wooed thee, Anne,
> Yet wooing thee, I found thee of more value
> Than stamps in gold or sums in sealed bags;
> And 'tis the very riches of thyself
> That now I aim at.

$$(3.4.13-18)$$

In other words, Fenton's initially mercenary motives change, as over the course of his wooing he becomes capable of distinguishing between the bags of coin, which now seem merely contingent, and Anne's intrinsic value, "the very riches of thyself." Once again, the terms "riches" and "value" both register the overlap and mark the dissimilarity between his initial intentions and his current ones: the same language of wealth is appropriate for both, but the references apparently diverge. Once again, verbal fuzziness or ambiguity here seems less a simple conviction that "you are what you own," an obliviousness to the distinction between person and property, than a sign of the entanglement of two theoretically and perhaps actually separable entities.

However intricate these entanglements may become, they do not exhaust the complexities of the property concept. So far I have been discussing property as if it involved only two terms, the "person" or proprietor on one hand, and the thing owned, possessed, or held in some way, on the other. And this has been, in fact, the way many recent scholars of early modern English culture have construed it, focusing upon garments, beds, portrait miniatures, joint-stools, pewter cups, linen napkins and so forth as *objects* (and as not-subjects). Yet focusing on *property* as opposed to *things* leads in a somewhat different methodological direction. For the concept of property works along two axes simultaneously: "vertically," so to speak, to designate a relationship between a thing and its owner, an "object" and a "subject," and also, at least as significantly, "horizontally" among human beings. Property rights are inherently social, asserted relative to other persons: to exclude trespassers, or designate heirs, or distinguish a hierarchy of claims by different persons to the same object or territory. Intuitions about property rights inform conceptions about what persons are entitled to, what they may be owed, what they are "worth" in obviously material and in not-so-material ways. Insofar as the suitable allocation of material resources is one of the provinces of justice, the concept of property thus inevitably engages with the domains of politics, ethics, and the law.[15]

In early modern England, the social complexities of proprietary relationships create dizzyingly multiple ways in which persons might relate to property, particularly property in land. If, as lawyers are fond of saying, property relations are best imagined as a "bundle of rights," English common law disaggregated those rights, distinguishing fee simple from fee tail and from copyhold, knight-service tenure from socage tenure, life estate from leasehold, usufruct from possession, ownership from seisin, incorporeal from corporeal things, real property from chattels (and both from the intermediate category, "real chattels").[16] Common lawyers simultaneously deployed two overlapping but incongruent systems of classifying property rights in land: the "tenures," which were categories that had developed over time, and the "estates," which were defined in functional, ahistorical terms.[17] Each of these property categories configures a different relation among persons, while at the same time specifying particular forms of intimacy and control between a proprietor and the thing he possesses.

In short, in the case of early modern England we are not confronted with a society in which fine discriminations in kinds of property right, or between property and person, are inconceivable or never made. Rather it seems that in some contexts, those discriminations are invoked, pursued, and elaborated to a mind-boggling degree, while in other contexts they can be cavalierly disregarded.

A second kind of complexity is less conceptual than historical. In the sixteenth century, the beginning of a transition from an agrarian to a mercantile economy entailed fairly rapid changes in perceptions of what possessions were considered necessary or desirable. William Harrison, writing in 1577, testifies to the increased luxury of home furnishings, "and herein I do not speak of the nobility and gentry only, but likewise of the lowest sort in most places of our south country." At table, pewter or even silver cups and eating utensils replaced wooden implements. In the bedchamber, sleepers now expected featherbeds, not straw mattresses, and soft pillows instead of "a good round log under their heads."[18] Modern economic historians have ratified Harrison's observation, pointing to England's nascent manufacturing sector, which was beginning to produce relatively cheaply items—pins, for instance—that previously had had to be imported at great expense.[19] What were once luxuries thus could become cheap and commonplace commodities. In elite circles, goods imported by England's newly active overseas trading sector became hallmarks of sophistication and taste: porcelain, silk, tapestries, oriental carpets. A higher standard of living involved not merely possessing more of everything, but often of having, or at least wanting, things different from those previously considered desirable. At the same time other commodities—firewood, for instance—that had once been widely available became scarce and dear; with the felling of the forests in southern England, first the London poor, and then the rich, resorted to heating their rooms and cooking their food with the dirtier, smellier soft coal shipped down the coast from northern England.[20] Rampant inflation over the course of the sixteenth century further complicated this change in the availability of various kinds of goods, by changing the quantum of labor required to purchase various common items. A variety of interrelated factors, therefore, combined to make questions of value seem disconcertingly unfixed in the early modern period.[21]

These epochal social and economic changes were taking place in a society with a largely precedent-based legal system, in which many of the relevant cases dated from the early Norman period. Generally it was easier to devise an elaborate legal fiction, jerry-rigging an accommodation with an archaic law, than to reform the legal code by statute. Moreover, the availability of multiple legal venues, each with its own procedures, gave plaintiffs a choice of systems, and they would naturally choose the one most beneficial to themselves. Gregory Kneidel draws a vivid analogy:

The terms and practices of early modern land law were constantly evolving to confront new threats, less like the current
collection of standardized forms with which most of us are
familiar and more like computer system software. Landholders
could choose what operating system to use—the common law,
like Windows, controlled but did not monopolize the market—
and these systems were constantly being updated to prevent
new virus threats, to add desirable new features, and to com-
pete better with other systems. Lawyers...could exploit the
flaws of the common-law system for their own and for their
clients' profit, or they could find that it was just as profitable
to work for the system: that is, to write security software to
protect it from other hackers.[22]

The result was, by Shakespeare's time, a considerable and ever-
widening gap between property law and actual practice, which
could render apparently established principles highly unstable or
even moot. Practice diverged quite drastically from what seems to
be the letter of the law in regard to entailments, or in regard to
women's inheritance and property rights. Indeed, Eileen Spring
argues:

Landowners had their rules, and the common law had its,
and they differed in every major respect. Legal history is a
long, multifaceted struggle against the common law rule of
inheritance...Indeed that the English law of real property is
of abnormal complexity is due to landowners' distaste for the
common law rules.[23]

Moreover, the researches of social historians have revealed that the
ways in which landholding peasants and town dwellers managed
and related to their property deviated markedly from the behavior
of large estate holders, even though they were all supposedly subject
to the "common" law.[24]

For scholars of Elizabethan and Jacobean drama, what might be
called a "generic source of error" further complicates the conceptual
and historical challenges of formulating a clear view of the relations
between property and persons. Works of literature have their limits
as evidence of an early modern *Weltanschauung*, in which, as some

materialist critics would have it, subject and object were supposedly in a more intimate, less contingent or alienated relation than they are today. A great deal of early modern drama, Shakespeare's included, deals with astonishing, emotionally charged, eventfully compressed, and, therefore, wildly unusual situations. Actual princesses do not flee to the greenwood in male disguise, there to court and marry indigent younger brothers; nor do slighted subordinates typically murder their daughters' rapists and bake them in pies; nor do affluent merchants sign bonds forfeiting pounds of their own flesh to vengeful usurers. The interest of such plots lies not in their mimetic scrupulousness but in their outrageous, and therefore exciting, flouting of expectation. Playwrights rarely if ever depict the purely instrumental buying, selling, or management of property, the setting up of trust arrangements in order to avoid taxation or to evade the law of coverture, the surveying of land, the nitty-gritty of prenuptial negotiations, the drafting of wills, or indeed any of the myriad humdrum transactions that preoccupy early modern notaries, executors, and attorneys. The staging of those transactions, absent any other motive, would seem impertinent or tedious: they are simply not what plays are supposed to be about, in early modern England or today. Thus it is not surprising—indeed, it practically follows from the nature of the theatrical enterprise—that "subject and object" should seem tightly connected in early modern drama, whatever might have been the case in other domains of endeavor. For were they not thus connected, the playwright would not have chosen to represent them in the first place. As Anton Chekhov famously advised: "If in the first act you have hung a pistol on the wall, then in the following one it should be fired. Otherwise don't put it there."[25] Life outside the theater fails to observe the same neat economy of means.

Despite, or more likely because, of these various complexities, many Renaissance dramatists—perhaps most obviously Ben Jonson, Thomas Dekker, Thomas Heywood, and Thomas Middleton in their city comedies—write play after play about the ways property relationships shape and distort relations among human beings. It is sometimes hard to know what *else* might be at issue in such plays as *The Alchemist, Bartholomew Fair, A Trick to Catch the Old One,* or *A Chaste Maid in Cheapside*. Shakespeare is not so single-minded. Because of the cornucopian richness of the Shakespearean text, it is probably possible for an ingenious interpreter to find traces of an engagement with property issues in a wide swathe of his plays. Very frequently, such concerns are of interest in passing: for instance, *As You Like It* briefly touches upon the distinction, in pastoral Arden, between the hired shepherd and the herdsman who owns his own flocks. In *Julius Caesar*, Antony's public reading of Caesar's will, bequeathing his wealth to the citizens of Rome, helps turns the populace against Caesar's assassins; Antony's cool abrogation of the legacies two scenes later showcases his cynical political shrewdness. Nonetheless, in comparison to the city-comedy playwrights, Shakespeare focuses intensely upon property concerns in rather intermittent fashion. In the mid-1590s, he writes the second tetralogy of history plays and *The Merchant of Venice*, plays which persistently return to questions about property and power, to issues of inheritance and prodigality, to the relationship between landed property and chattel property, to the way property concerns are intertwined with various kinds of social alliances and intimacies. About ten years later, he writes *King Lear* and *Timon of Athens*, both of which centrally concern themselves with what happens when somebody gives away everything that he possesses. I shall be examining some of these plays, in which property issues play a prominent, virtually unavoidable, role, in the chapters that follow.

Shakespeare's imagined worlds, while taking early modern regimes of property as a point of departure, freely invent, simplify, and exaggerate particular features of those regimes, in what might be called a "poetics of property." The details of his poetry of property vary considerably from play to play,[26] sometimes even from one part to another of the same play, in a way that cannot be deduced from some generalized materialist privileging of objects over subjects, or on the other hand by attention to the arcana of Elizabethan property law, but only by close attention to what is happening and what is uttered in a particular situation.

It is this poetics of property that will comprise the subject of this book. Some materialist critics, as I have already noted, have decried the narcissism of a criticism focused on human beings, on "subjects" as opposed to "objects." My own approach is, however, unashamedly anthropocentric. Plays are written by human beings, for human beings, about human beings. As I've mentioned, property relations are not merely ways of attaching "persons" to "things," "subjects" to "objects," but are a careful distribution of rights and obligations among persons. The study of the way property is deployed in Shakespeare plays turns out to be a study less of things than of relationships mediated by things: between prince and subject, master and servant, parent and child, siblings, friends, and enemies.

Let us return to *Richard II*. There is a long tradition of considering this play as the juncture at which Shakespeare broke from his own previous historical drama and from the precedent set by Marlowe's *Edward II*, and discovered new techniques of characterization that would eventually inform his mature tragedies. Several critics have thus seen *Richard II* in teleological terms, as an embryonic *Hamlet*.[27] At the same time, the play involves itself, as I have already noted, very deeply with property claims. It is therefore a good place to embark upon a consideration of property concerns in Shakespeare, and of whether and how those concerns might be tied up with questions of dramatic characterization.

When the Duke of York chastises Bolingbroke for defying his sentence of exile and returning home prematurely, Bolingbroke defends himself stoutly. He comes, he says, to assert his property rights.

> Will you permit that I shall stand condemned
> A wandering vagabond, my rights and royalties
> Plucked from my arms perforce and given away
> To upstart unthrifts? Wherefore was I born?
> If that my cousin King be King in England
> It must be granted I am Duke of Lancaster.
>
> (2.3.118–23).

Bolingbroke makes several interesting and tendentious assertions in these lines. One is that by seizing the inheritance to which he is entitled, Richard has robbed him not merely of land but of a political identity, even a *raison d'etre*: "Wherefore was I born?" In Bolingbroke's view, tit : to the peerage—the fact that Bolingbroke is Duke of Lancaster—necessarily entails possession of the ducal lands, so that the King's seizure of the one is the same as the seizure of the other. Plucking the lands, with their associated rights and royalties, from his arms, in the sense of his grasp, is thus the same as stripping him of his coat of arms, the heraldry that proclaims him the son of John of Gaunt, the previous Duke of Lancaster.[28] Moreover, Bolingbroke asserts that his proprietary right to the duchy of Lancaster is analogous to Richard's claim to be king of England: that the monarchy is itself a kind of proprietary right in land, the land in question being the entire kingdom. York himself had earlier given voice to a similar conception when he objected to Richard's seizure of Lancaster:

> Take Hereford's rights away, and take from Time
> His charters and his customary rights:
> Let not tomorrow then ensue today;
> Be not thyself, for how art thou a king
> But by fair sequence and succession?

>   (2.1.196–200)

Both Bolingbroke and York, in other words, imagine the king's political role as a form of property right; the monarchy inherited in "fair sequence" by "charters and customary rights" just as acreage and title are inherited by any landed proprietor. Conversely, they construe landholding as a form of political authority.

At first glance this conflation may seem erroneous. Since Roman times, lawyers and political philosophers had distinguished between what they called *imperium*, or the governing power of the magistrate, and *dominium*, or the power of a proprietor over the things he owned. The distinction, however, was necessary in the first place because sovereignty and ownership were closely related concepts. As Kevin Gray and Susan Francis Gray write in their essay, "The Idea of Property in Land":

> Property is...the word used to describe particular concentrations of power *over* things and resources. The term "property" is simply an abbreviated reference to a quantum of socially permissible power exercised in respect of a socially valued resource.[29]

Because property rights and sovereignty seem not different sorts of power-to-control, but different degrees or aspects of the same power, the distinction between *dominium* and *imperium*, as the Grays demonstrate, was an imprecise one. Some classical authorities, for instance, drew the *imperium/dominium* distinction not between persons and things but rather between political and domestic relations. They considered the rule of a husband over wife, children, and slaves a form of *dominium*, insofar as the authority relations in question were familial rather than public. Conversely large-scale property ownership seems inevitably to assume some of the characteristics of political power.

If property rights, especially the property rights of very wealthy persons, always seem analogous in some way to political sovereignty, the analogy is even tighter, and the distinction between the two forms of power even muddier, in medieval Europe. The property at issue in *Richard II* is "real" or landed property: in an agrarian society, not merely one of many interchangeable forms of wealth, but a privileged category insofar as it is the literal ground of wealth, the material from which, under cultivation, abundance can be generated. In medieval and early modern England, nobody technically "owns" land in the sense of having *dominium* over it. Rather, a proprietor "holds" the land—called a "fee"—"of" a lord in return for stipulated services or payments. He is thus called a "tenant" [Fr. "holder"] rather than an "owner," and his right to the land is called "seisin." In other words, medieval and early modern land law imagines territory less as a personal possession than as a strategic grant from lord to vassal. In the years immediately following the Norman Conquest, great landholders might be obliged to maintain a force of armed men as a condition of the land grant; by Richard II's time the obligation had been converted to a money payment. In either case the land was supposed to provide the vassal with necessary means for performing that service or mustering that support: the more significant the service, the larger the tract of land.

The medieval and early modern system of land tenure thus invested landholders, and especially tenants-in-chief who held directly of the king, with political roles inextricable with their rights in land. Carol Rose notes the tight connection between a feudal nobleman's real property, inherited from his father, and his "proper," likewise inherited, social role:

That "property" was the mainstay of "propriety" was a quite common understanding before the seventeenth and eighteenth centuries... This version of property did *not* envision property as a set of tradable and ultimately interchangeable goods; instead, different kinds of property were associated with different kinds of roles.[30]

Not only the king but his more important vassals possessed not merely the rights to "enjoy" their territories, but political power over those who inhabit that territory. In medieval England, and despite the increasing power of the monarch in early modern England, even in Shakespeare's time, the great landholders wielded significant authority over the regions they controlled. Lower down the social scale, the landed gentry customarily served as justices of the peace, and the manorial "courts leet" tried, convicted, and punished petty criminals. Although it is possible to distinguish the role of landholder from the role of magistrate, as Roman law had distinguished between *dominium* and *imperium*, in ordinary circumstances political authority comes with the territory, so to speak. We see this assumption in Gaunt's famous description of England:

> This royal throne of kings, this sceptered isle,
> This earth of majesty, this seat of Mars,
> This other Eden, demi-paradise,
> This fortress built by nature for herself
> Against infection and the hand of war,
> This happy breed of men, this little world...
>
> (2.1.40–5)

All but one of these epithets refer, more or less literally, to England as a *place*: "throne," "isle," "earth," "seat," "paradise," "fortress," "world." "Happy breed of men" doesn't seem to fit, insofar as it describes not the land but the people who live on it. For Gaunt, though, this is normally a distinction without a difference. The king's "realm" is both a geographical domain and a group of persons organized into a polity. The concepts are intertwined for the king's chief vassals as well: their names are the names of their dukedoms and earldoms,

because these territories are what endow them with a political identity. When York accuses the newly returned Bolingbroke of not
having observed the terms of his sentence—"Thou art a banished
man, and here art come | Before the expiration of thy time"—Bol-
ingbroke replies, "As I was banished, I was banished Hereford,| But
as I come, I come for Lancaster" (2.3.109–13). Coming *for* Lancaster
means coming *as* "Lancaster," refusing to acknowledge persons who
address him by his former name, as Berkeley innocently does in Act
2 scene 3, until they remedy their error by affording him the correct
honorific. In Act 3 scene 1 he has Bushy and Green beheaded for
having, among other offenses, torn his coat of arms out of the windows of his houses. Erasing the family inscription, they have treated
the estate in land as if it were an ordinary economic asset that could
be freely transferred from one proprietor to another. This is, according to Bolingbroke, a capital error.[31]

Landed property was thus profoundly enmeshed in prescribed
relationships of hierarchy and reciprocation between status groups—
lords and vassals—but in a double-sided way. On the one hand, the
tenant of a fee owed homage to his lord as a condition of his tenure,
so the existence of the tenure testified to his subordination. On the
other hand, the tenure also provided the feeholder a material basis
for independence, especially after legal developments in the twelfth
and thirteenth centuries bolstered the rights of the tenant against the
rights of the lord, ensuring the heritability of the fee and permitting
some land to be alienated without the lord's consent. A feeholder
who controlled a wealth-generating estate did not depend for his
support upon the whim of the monarch. That estate might serve
passively as a refuge, a zone of retirement if the lord's importunities
become too unbearable; moreover, the wherewithal to raise an
armed power could be—and fairly often, was—turned to rebellion
as well as to the king's service. Thus the feeholder's right to free
enjoyment of the land gave him the practical means to resist monar-
chical authority, and it is in recognition of the subversive potential
of those resources that the punishment for treason included not
merely death but the forfeiture to the Crown of the traitor's land
rights, and thus the disinheritance of his heirs.[32] Because of the way
landholding bolstered a degree of self-sufficiency, landless persons
were long considered politically incompetent; those reliant upon

wages, the theory went, could not resist the importunities of their employers and thus were not capable of operating as sufficiently free political agents.[33] Indeed twenty-first century defenses of private property make the same connection among proprietary rights, personal liberty, and political agency, though nowadays the original prestige of land is well-nigh forgotten.

So in the medieval and early modern period landed property both knits different status groups together in a relation of mutual support, and at the same time separates them by clearly defining their respective roles. It underwrites political power, permitting the wealthy and the well-born to assert their authority over others, but at the same time it is the means by which political power can be constrained and resisted. The oath-taking of vassalage is designed to harmonize the potentially distinct interests of lord and vassal in landed property. It produces a government by implicit consent rather than by raw coercion, and structures sovereign power in terms not only of control but of limits to control.

As I have already noted, in *Richard II* the immediate trigger of rebellion is Richard's appropriation of the Lancastrian estates. In fact, a fee routinely reverted back to the lord upon the death of its tenant, so Richard is not wrong to take possession of the land; what is wrong is his refusal to yield it to the tenant's heir when the heir "sues his livery," that is, tenders the entry fine and declares his readiness to take a loyalty oath. Provided the conditions of homage are performed, the descent is Bolingbroke's by right, not subject to the lord's discretion. Bolingbroke thus complains:

> I am denied to sue my livery here,
> And yet my letters patent give me leave.
> . . .
> What would you have me do? I am a subject,
> And I challenge law; attorneys are denied me;
> And therefore personally I lay my claim
> To my inheritance of free descent.

> (2.3.128–35)

Bolingbroke represents his return from exile not, initially, as the repudiation of his subjection to Richard but rather as a frustrated, first-person attempt to *insist* upon that subjection: a subordination which legally guarantees the "free descent" of his father's estate. He carefully makes a legal case for his defiance of the law: he is trying desperately, he claims, to follow proper procedures.

Yet Bolingbroke comes not merely in person, but at the head of an army. His support comes from those injured by Richard's previous offenses against his subjects' property rights. Details of these unpopular policies are bruited about early in the play. The dying Gaunt, chastising Richard, contrasts the quasi-Edenic England of his own youth with the degenerate England of the present, which is, he complains, "now leased out...Like to a tenement or pelting farm" (2.1.59–60). Later in the same scene he reiterates the accusation: "It were a shame to let this land by lease....Landlord of England art thou now, now king" (2.1.110, 113). What is it about the leasing of property that so outrages Gaunt? A leasehold differs from a "fee," or feudal grant, in that it is a purely contractual, time-limited bargain that does not establish a political relationship between lord and vassal. It imposes feudal obligations neither upon lessor nor lessee, and its terms are fixed not by custom but according to mutual consent and to the conditions of the market. According to Gaunt, Richard has treated his land purely as an economic resource, maximizing its profit to himself without regard to a feudal lord's responsibility to his subjects and their thriving.[34] By reducing land to simply another form of economic capital, Richard's behavior deprives land of its relationship to tradition and history, and denies landholders— including, potentially, himself—the special political status that they are accustomed to possess in a feudal system. Thus, in Gaunt's view, Richard undermines his own status as ultimate feudal overlord.

Gaunt's complaint echoes language Richard uses in the previous scene. "We are enforced to farm our royal realm," Richard admits, "The revenue whereof shall furnish us | For our affairs in hand" (1.4.44–6). But the echo may be misleading, because Richard often uses the word "farm" in a different sense from Gaunt. "Farming" could signify the leasing out of land to investors who pay rent to the titleholder—the behavior that apparently offends Gaunt. It could also refer to the sale of the king's taxation prerogative to a delegate, who collected the tax plus an overage to compensate himself for his own labor. This seems to be the "farming" that Richard has in mind, as his further comments reveal. On the verge of leaving for Ireland, he announces: "Our substitutes at home shall have blank charters. | Whereto, when they shall know what men are rich, | They shall subscribe them for large sums of gold | And send them after to supply our wants" (1.4. 47–50). In Richard's cavalier formulation, the tax farm seems to become a technically legal form of theft.

So in *Richard II*, the word "farm" actually indicates two distinct endeavors, which have in common that they seem to be forms of shady practice deployed to increase the king's revenue stream by delegating his traditional prerogatives. In fact, though, the air of impropriety that hangs over the practice of "farming," in both these senses, is a little mysterious. By the late middle ages the leasing of land was a well-established practice and remained ubiquitous in Shakespeare's time. Its advantages were flexibility for both the lease-holder and the titleholder, conducive to more efficient land use than the rigid categories of feudal tenure. At the same time, feudal tenure was evolving away from the rather simple system established in the years following the Conquest. Originally the king granted land to his vassals in return for knight-service, that is, the obligation of the vassal to raise a corps of soldiers and come to the military aid of his lord in time of need. By Richard II's time, knight-service had been converted, in many cases, to money payments, an arrangement called socage tenure. Socage tenure was more convenient for both king and vassal, and moreover contributed to the peace of the realm, by discouraging powerful magnates from maintaining armies of men who owed allegiance to individual noblemen rather than to the monarch.[35] Socage and leaseholding remained legally distinct categories, and socage tenure, unlike the leasehold, was always heritable. Yet in fact both turned on a similar exchange of money payment for the right to occupy and take the profits of cultivated land. In addition, over the centuries leaseholders gradually gained rights virtually identical to those of the socage tenant, so the distinction between the two forms grew finer still, producing by Shakespeare's time what A. W. B. Simpson calls "a very confused body of law" attempting to describe the precise differences.[36] The substitution of cash rents for knight-service may well have had, as Gaunt notes, the effect of dis-aggregating proprietary rights in land from status and generational hierarchies, and of dividing economic from political obligations. But if so, the fault lies not with the lease per se, but with developments in land law and in practical governance that by the late fourteenth century had been in the works for hundreds of years.

Similarly, the tax farm was a routine arrangement prior to the existence of large-scale government bureaucracies: delegating tax collection to agents, who compensated themselves out of the collected proceeds, was an accepted way to get the job done. Tax farming had been employed all over Europe since Roman imperial times, and continued to flourish in Shakespeare's day, providing Elizabeth's favorites with some of their most lucrative emoluments. Thus Elizabeth awarded the Earl of Leicester the customs farm on silk, velvet, oils, currants, and sweet wine; after Leicester's death the farm of sweet wine was awarded to Essex. (Elizabeth's revocation of this arrangement in 1600, which brought Essex to the verge of bankruptcy, was a precipitating factor in his revolt.) Richard may well exploit the tax farm much further than is prudent—Elizabeth, by contrast, farmed the customs taxes on imported luxury goods, which were never subject to Parliamentary approval and which were levied only on notionally optional purchases. On the other hand, Richard needs revenue in order to fight a war, a budget item for which kings had always been permitted to tax their subjects.

The problem, then, is perhaps not that Richard is doing anything especially egregious for a king, but rather that royal power itself is dangerously unstable. On the one hand the king's power is sustained by his vassal's secure property rights; on the other hand the security of those rights, particularly the right of heirs to "take" or inherit regardless of the feudal lord's interests, reinforces the power of the landholder against the lord, and in particular the power of tenants-in-chief against the king. As I have already suggested, the ideology that supported the feudal system is one of elaborate harmony and mutual support, but in fact, multiple-layered claims over the same piece of territory create the possibility of conflict between those layers. If the conflicts are resolved in favor of the feeholder, he who has seisin to an estate in land, then the rights of the overlord are necessarily restricted, and vice versa. Hence the importance of established law and precedent to restrain the self-aggrandizement of individuals, to regulate what would otherwise be their "mere will" or "lusts," and to restore, according to socially acceptable principles, the functioning of each facet within a complex social array. In Gaunt's view, leaseholding and tax farming rupture the tight connection between political and proprietary relationships, making too blatant the King's self-seeking and thus opening up an obvious chasm between his interests and the interests of his subjects. Yet in a system in which *dominium* and *imperium* already overlap, the only way to close that chasm is to limit, severely and perhaps fatally, the King's options and thus constrain his authority over his subjects.

This double bind produces an interesting double vision of Richard's dilemma, one as seen from the King's point of view, the other from the subject's, which pervades the discussion of Richard's culpability in Shakespeare's source, Holinshed's *Chronicles*. Richard is on the one hand berated as tyrannical: "neither law, justice, nor equity could take place, where the King's willful will was bent upon any wrongful purpose." On the other hand, he is elsewhere described as more sinned against than sinning: "he was a prince the most unthankfully used of his subjects, of any one of whom ye shall lightly read."[37] Shakespeare, of course, inherits and builds upon this ambivalence, simultaneously blaming Richard for his unaccountable stupidities, and soliciting pity for him as intolerably wronged.

Which comes first: property-holding or political power? Gaunt and York assume that royal power is founded upon, modeled upon, rights to landed property. Yet while both of them are generally regarded as the consciences or prophetic voices of the play, in fact the principle they articulate is a controversial one—not a simple statement of fact but the self-interested formulation of powerful landholders within a monarchy, poised both as subordinate to, and in some respects independent from, their king. The effect of imagining sovereignty as a form of property-holding is to imagine the sovereign as constrained by human rules and precedents, just as the landholder is. This view of royal power is at variance with the other understanding of monarchy in the play, in which the king is instituted by God and thus responsible to God alone. The latter conception is expressed in the sacred ceremony of anointing with holy oil, which does not so much create legitimacy as acknowledge a hierarchical relationship that God has supposedly already mandated.

Early in the play, this mystical conception of kingship is still strong: it restrains Gaunt from revenge, and encourages Richard to believe that

> Not all the water in the rough rude sea
> Can wash the balm from an anointed king.
> The breath of worldly men cannot depose
> The deputy elected by the Lord.

> (3.2.50–3)

Even after Bolingbroke has effectively seized power, the Bishop of Carlisle may stubbornly object that it is unseemly and impious for "subject and inferior breath" to presume to judge "the figure of God's majesty, | His captain, steward, deputy elect, | Anointed, crowned, planted many years" (4.1. 116–19). "What subject can give sentence on his king?" (4.1.112)—for the Bishop this is a rhetorical question, to which the answer is, "no subject." Yet the apparent impunity with which Bolingbroke operates—the silence of the supposedly offended divinity, or at least his slowness to react—seems implicitly to ratify a more pragmatic, less theological conception of monarchy.

Must the king operate within a constraining system of laws, or does his power exceed, indeed create, those laws? This point was unsettled in Richard's time, and remained unsettled in Shakespeare's. Yet the play suggests that when push comes to shove, the "monarch-as-legally-constrained-landholder" model trumps that of "monarch-as-anointed-delegate-of-God". It is certainly the view that eventually prevails as a matter of fact.

The analysis of royal power in *Richard II* as, essentially, an exalted form of feudal landholding implies an extremely tight connection between being and having, or at least between ruling and having. Yet that's not the play's whole story. For if the institutions of feudal land tenure tend to conflate property-holding, sovereign authority, and personal identity, the plot of *Richard II* pulls them apart. The play is, after all, about a usurpation—about wresting a "realm" and all that it entails in territory and human beings away from one title-holder and conferring it upon another. If being king and having a kingdom were completely inseparable—if the realm were, so to speak, permanently soldered to the monarch—usurpation would be an impossibility. Indeed, Richard at first entertains this scenario, suggesting that his land will rise up against and expel the rebel:

> This earth shall have a feeling, and these stones
> Prove armed soldiers, ere her native king
> Shall falter under foul rebellion's arms.
>
> (3.2.24–6)

Even as he articulates this hope, however, he apologizes for its implausibility: "Mock not my senseless conjuration, lords" (3.2.22). He calls the conjuration "senseless" both because he knows that it is unlikely to happen and because, even while characterizing his earth as beloved child and loyal servant, he knows it does not, actually, "have a feeling" or hear his plea: the land as well as the conjuration is "senseless." As the play continues, what had initially seemed like a tight bundle of rights and perquisites starts to unravel. In other words, *Richard II* initially presents a world in which you are what you own, and you rule what you own, and those equations simply seem to be ingrained in the world. Yet after Bolingbroke's successful invasion, the original paradigm no longer holds.

The transfer of kingship from Richard to Henry is synecdochically represented in a royal horse, first mentioned by York in his account to his Duchess of Bolingbroke's triumphant entrance into London. The "hot and fiery steed" upon which Bolingbroke is mounted seems to recognize his rider, claims York; and Bolingbroke's ability to manage the spirited animal in the crowded London streets, holding him to a slow walk while meanwhile addressing his cheering subjects in complimentary terms, apparently bespeaks his natural fitness for rule. Skillful horsemanship was a traditional symbol of royal authority and military power as well as the self-government of the passions, and Shakespeare evokes it often in these connections: we will encounter it again in the *Henry IV* plays and *Henry V*. Yet in a short vignette close to the end of the play, Richard and a Groom who has visited him in prison discuss the same horse in more familiar terms. The animal turns out to have a name, Barbary, which—like the names of many of the human beings in the play—is a place name that designates a noble lineage. He is evidently one of the purebred "Arabian" horses imported from the coast of North Africa (Barbary) during and after the Crusades to improve northern European bloodstocks. Beautiful, swift, and extremely valuable, Barbary is a suitable mount for a monarch: a walking, or prancing, advertisement of kingly puissance. In the past, Richard has favored Barbary with personal attention, petting him and hand-feeding him bread. But while the Groom retains his memory of and loyalty to Richard, the horse does not. Now the property of Boling-broke, he goes, the Groom reports, "So proudly as if he disdained the ground" (5.5.83): just as splendid under one claimant as under another. The sense of personal connection that Richard had cherished, and that York had attempted to discern in the horse's comportment under Bolingbroke, is simply illusory. Like the rest of Richard's realm, the horse is "senseless." The possession that seemed most intimately linked to and expressive of Richard's identity as king, as "England," is—literally—a foreign body, as remote as the Barbary Coast. The horse, then, seems to embody the paradox of property as *Richard II* conceives it.

What happens to the King when he is separated from the possessions that originally seemed to sustain—even to constitute—him? We see the rupture opening up in the deposition scene, Act 4 scene 1, when Bolingbroke objects to Richard's theatrics: "I thought you had been willing to resign." Richard's reply complicates the relationship between emotional states and property even while asserting an analogy between them:

> BOLINGBROKE   I thought you had been willing to resign.
> RICHARD   My crown I am, but still my griefs are mine.
>   You may my glories and my state depose,
>   But not my griefs: still am I king of those.
> BOLINGBROKE   Part of your cares you give me with your crown.
> RICHARD   Your cares set up do not pluck my cares down.
>   My care is loss of care by old care done;
>   You care is gain of care by new care won.
>   The cares I give I have, though given away;
>   They 'tend the crown, yet still with me they stay.

$$(4.1.180-9)$$

"Cares" and "griefs" obey neither the social rules governing the bestowal of gifts, nor the physical laws that confine material objects to a single specifiable location, nor the legal precepts that regulate ordinary transfers of ownership.

Because of this lack of correlation between "cares and griefs" and such material objects as crown and scepter, the vanishing of propri-etary rights turns out not to be the same as the vanishing of the person, despite Richard's sometimes fervent wish that the two were more neatly aligned. The deposition scene, in which he formally relinquishes power to Bolingbroke, repeatedly echoes the last scene of Marlowe's *Doctor Faustus*. "O soul, be changed to little water drops," Faustus cries, "And fall into the ocean, ne'er be found." Richard wishes: "O, that I were a mockery king of snow, | Stand-ing before the sun of Bolingbroke | To melt myself away in water drops" (4.1.250–2). Both Faustus and Richard yearn for personal dissolution and recoil from the idea that they must persist, but per-sist they must and do. And Richard's persistence is the more theat-rically consequential, since Faustus' despairing wish for utter annihilation is only a few lines before the end of the play, while Richard's deposition scene comes at the beginning of the fourth act. We will have two acts in which to consider what it means that Richard has not melted away like a snowman in the sun. What does it mean, the play seems to ask, to continue to exist after everything that seems "proper" to one's identity has been stripped away?

Interestingly, the moment at which Richard relinquishes his king-dom is the moment at which he has seemed, to so many readers and audiences, to come into himself most fully as a character.[38] Critics who dislike Richard often complain about his recklessly self-destruc-tive "histrionic" personality, as if he seems to think the world well lost if only he gets a good soliloquy out of it, and within the play Richard's allies, his queen and Aumerle, complain about his prefer-ence for bewailing and analyzing his fate rather than taking decisive action. Yet what seems like maximum disempowerment and humili-ation is also, from another perspective, a kind of subjective triumph. That's surely the point of the pervasive comparison between Rich-ard and Jesus in the last couple of acts; Richard draws on a long ascetic Christian tradition in which the deepest truths are found not in possession but in radical and complete renunciation. "Ay, no, no, ay, for I must nothing be," Richard asserts: the "ay," both "yes" and the first person singular pronoun, is the opposite of "no," and at the same time "no" seems to be its enabling condition. Full of the grief and care that he cannot transfer to another, Richard asserts that they alone are irrevocably his, and him:

> my grief lies all within,
> And these external manner of laments
> Are merely shadows to the unseen grief
> That swells with silence in the tortured soul.
> There lies the substance...

(4.1.285–9)

It is this interior turn that permits us to see Richard II as Hamlet's predecessor, one who has that within which passes show.

Still, in yet another turn of the screw, Richard's subjective complexity might be seen not so much an abjuring of property as its introjection. Early in the play, Gaunt introduces language that conflates the king's having with his being:

> A thousand flatterers sit within thy crown
> Whose compass is no bigger than thy head.
> And yet, encaged in so small a verge,
> The waste is no whit lesser than thy land.

(2.1.100–3)

The dying Gaunt speaks "as a prophet new inspired" and the action of the play eventually literalizes what is here a vertiginous analogy between the inside of the King's head and his external dominions. In the last two acts of *Richard II*, roles normally distributed among various agents in a social array collapse into a single individual, and that individual is Richard.

This conflation might be seen as a fitting punishment for the King's earlier solipsistic or narcissistic behavior: having ignored the claims of his subjects in favor of his own "will" and "lusts," Richard is now left alone with only his will and lusts as company, personified as the subjects of an imaginary kingdom. At the same time, it's

difficult for *Richard II*'s audience to experience this collapse as an
entirely negative or punitive event, because the fact that the titular
hero must now play all roles himself is precisely what makes him
seem theatrically fascinating: complex, contradictory, layered, paradoxical. In Richard's final soliloquy, isolated in prison, forcibly
separated from his queen, bereft of his kingdom and denied his
procreative futurity, he puzzles over the apparently contradictory
Scriptural passages on the relationship between wealth and salva-
tion, generating thereby a populous world from his "still-breeding
thoughts": "Thus play I in one person many people, | And none
contented" (5.5.31–2).The King carries the whole realm in his own
head, but arguably only a radical form of dispossession has made
manifest the intrinsically "proper." For it's only in the moment of
dispossession that property becomes openly and purely a function
of the imagination. In an irony that *Richard II* shares with many if
not all tragedies, wrenching loss is the prerequisite for its hero becoming consequential as the topic of a story. Threatened by Bolingbroke's invasion, Richard predicts both his dispossession and his
entry into fable:

> Our lands, our lives, and all are Bolingbroke's;
> And nothing we can call our own but death.
>   ...
> For God's sake, let us sit upon the ground,
> And tell sad stories of the death of kings –
> How some have been deposed, some slain in war,
> Some haunted by the ghosts they have deposed,
> Some poisoned by their wives, some sleeping killed,
> All murdered.

$$(3.2.147–56)$$

What had initially seemed scandalously exceptional—treason and
violence erupting upon an unsuspecting and peaceful land—now
turns out to be routine, the fate of all kings, or at least of all kings
of whom stories are told. Later in the play Richard once again imagines himself becoming a character in a tale his queen will tell in a
future "winter's tedious night," in another country. "Tell thou the
lamentable fall of me," he urges her, even as he parts with her

forever (5.1.44). In other words, in *Richard II*, the deposed king seems to console himself with the thought that his suffering makes him unforgettable, a proper topic for legend, and by the same token, his subjective complexity and "literary" distinctiveness seem to require worldly loss.

So, in *Richard II* is being a form of having, or is it not? Ay, no, no, ay, as Richard might say. When property is traumatically stripped away, the complex individual character remains—indeed, *it is possibly only in that deprivation that he is constituted as a complex individual character*. In the second half of the play, Richard's subjectivity is predicated not upon possession, but upon loss of possession. And yet Richard's mental complexity persistently structures itself on just the property regime it needs to forsake. The alternatives the play presents are either the helpless nostalgia of Gaunt and York, or despair, as articulated by Richard, who is left with a subjectivity that is predicated upon a contradiction. "Ay, no, no, ay": the conditions for self-realization are also the conditions in which the self cannot, apparently, exist. There seems to be no way out at the end of the play: Richard's final soliloquy shows him at an impasse, physically immobilized and with the same thoughts simply going round and round in his head.

And yet, of course, there is a way out, though not for Richard, and not in this play but in its sequels. What actually ensues is not a restoration of the former property regime but a new arrangement, and that will be the topic of the next chapter.

Notes

1 Jonathan Gil Harris, *Untimely Matter in the Time of Shakespeare* (Philadelphia, PA: University of Pennsylvania Press, 2009), p. 1.
2 Some exemplary books are: Margreta De Grazia, Maureen Quilligan, and Peter Stallybrass, eds., *Subject and Object in Renaissance Culture* (Cambridge: Cambridge University Press, 1996); Patricia Fumerton and Simon Hunt, eds., *Renaissance Culture and the Everyday* (Philadelphia, PA: University of Pennsylvania Press, 1999); Ann Rosalind Jones and Peter Stallybrass, *Renaissance Clothing and the Materials of Memory* (Cambridge: Cambridge University Press, 2000); Natasha Korda, *Shakespeare's Domestic Economies: Gender and Property in Early Modern England* (Philadelphia, PA: University of Pennsylvania Press, 2002); Jonathan Gil Harris and Natasha Korda, eds., *Staged Properties in Early Modern English Drama* (Cambridge:

Cambridge University Press, 2002); Julian Yates, *Error Misuse Failure: Object Lessons from the English Renaissance* (Minneapolis, MN: University of Minnesota Press, 2003); Andrew Sofer, *The Stage Life of Props* (Ann Arbor, MI: University of Michigan Press, 2004); Harris, *Untimely Matter in the Time of Shakespeare*. It is striking how much of this work has been produced by faculty at the University of Pennsylvania English Department and their former graduate students, or published by the University of Pennsylvania Press.

3 Peter Stallybrass, "The Value of Culture and the Disavowal of Things," in Henry S. Turner, ed., *The Culture of Capital: Property, Cities, and Knowledge in Early Modern England* (New York: Routledge, 2002), pp. 275–92 (p. 276).

4 Yates, *Error Misuse Failure*, p. 1. Althusser is sometimes cited in support of this theory, but this particular argument seems to impart to material objects, such as items of clothing, the interpellating power that Althusser assigns to ideology. For instance, Ann Rosalind Jones and Peter Stallybrass write: "Clothes...inscribe themselves upon a person who comes into being through that inscription. To understand the significance of clothes in the Renaissance, we need to undo our own social categories, in which subjects are prior to objects, wearers to what is worn. We need to understand the animatedness of clothes, their ability to 'pick up' subjects, to mold and shape them both physically and socially, to constitute subjects through their power." *Renaissance Clothing and the Materials of Memory*, p. 2.

5 Jones and Stallybrass, *Renaissance Clothing and the Materials of Memory*, p. 8.

6 Margreta de Grazia, "The Ideology of Superfluous Things: *King Lear* as Period Piece," in de Grazia, Quilligan, and Stallybrass, eds., *Subject and Object in Renaissance Culture*, pp. 17–42 (pp. 21–2, 25).

7 Margreta de Grazia, *Hamlet Without Hamlet* (Cambridge: Cambridge University Press, 2007), p. zz.

8 Sir William Blackstone, *Commentaries on the Laws of England*, ii: Of the Rights of Things (London; T. Cadell and W. Davies, 1809), p. 1.

9 David Hawkes, "Materialism and Reification in Renaissance Studies," *Journal of Early Modern Cultural Studies* 4 (2004): 114–29 (116).

10 Oliver Wendell Holmes, "The Path of Law," *Harvard Law Review* 10 (1897): 457–78.

11 See, e.g., *Euthydemus* 279–81, *Philebus* 48E–49A, *Laws* 743E.

12 *Laws* 742E–743C in Plato, *Complete Works*, ed. John M. Cooper (Indianapolis, IN: Hackett, 1997).

13 As, indeed, it remains: see, for instance, many of the essays in William Schweiker and Charles Mathewes, eds., *Having: Property and Possession in Religious and Social Life* (Grand Rapids, MI: Eerdmans, 2004).

14 de Grazia, "*King Lear* as Period Piece," p. 31.

15 There is a rich literature, so far little consulted by "materialist" scholars of early modern England, in the fields of law and political philosophy

on the concept of property. Much of this work is focused on the United States and is understandably concerned with hot topics in our own day—environmental protection, mineral rights, zoning, intellectual property, "the takings clause," and so forth—and as a result its analytical categories cannot simply be transferred wholesale onto the different historical circumstances of the Elizabethan and Jacobean periods. Nonetheless, the sophistication of this writing can helpfully illuminate the complexity of the property-concept. See, e.g., Bruce A. Ackerman, *Private Property and the Constitution* (New Haven, CT: Yale University Press, 1977); Lawrence C. Becker, *Property Rights—Philosophic Foundations* (London: Routledge, 1977); C. B. Macpherson, ed., *Property: Mainstream and Critical Traditions* (Toronto: University of Toronto Press, 1978); Steven Munzer, *A Theory of Property* (Cambridge: Cambridge University Press, 1990); Jennifer Nedelsky, *Private Property and the Limits of American Constitutionalism: The Madisonian Framework and Its Legacy* (Chicago, IL: University of Chicago Press, 1990); Margaret Radin, *Reinterpreting Property* (Chicago, IL: University of Chicago Press, 1993); Carol Rose, *Property and Persuasion: Essays on the History, Theory, and Rhetoric of Ownership* (Boulder, CO: Westview Press, 1994); J. W. Harris, *Property and Justice* (Oxford: Clarendon Press, 1996); J. E. Penner, *The Idea of Property in Law* (Oxford: Clarendon Press, 1997); Joseph William Singer, *Entitlement: The Paradoxes of Property* (New Haven, CT: Yale University Press, 2000); Laura Underkuffler, *The Idea of Property: Its Meaning and Power* (Oxford: Oxford University Press, 2003); Jedediah Purdy, *The Meaning of Property: Freedom, Community, and the Legal Imagination* (New Haven, CT: Yale University Press, 2010); Gregory S. Alexander and Eduardo M. Penalver, eds., *Property and Community* (Oxford: Oxford University Press, 2010).

16 For a magisterial survey of the complex law of real property in medieval and early modern England, intelligibly describing its original form and the ways it was modified over the centuries by statute and by legal fictions, see A. W. B. Simpson, *A History of the Land Law*, second edition (Oxford: Clarendon Press, 1986).

17 Eric Kerridge, *Agrarian Problems in the Sixteenth Century and After* (New York: Barnes and Noble, 1969), pp. 32–64.

18 William Harrison, *A Description of England*, ed. Georges Edelen (Ithaca, NY: Cornell University Press, 1968), pp. 200–3.

19 Joan Thirsk, *Economic Policy and Projects: The Development of a Consumer Society in Early Modern England* (Oxford: Clarendon Press, 1978); see also L. A. Clarkson, *The Pre-Industrial Economy in England 1500–1750* (London: Batsford, 1971).

20 Keith Wrightson, *Earthly Necessities: Economic Lives in Early Modern Britain* (New Haven, CT: Yale University Press, 2002).

21 For good discussions of the literary implications of the crisis of value in late sixteenth and early seventeenth century England, see Lars Engle, *Shakespearean Pragmatism: Market of His Time* (Chicago. IL: University of

Chicago Press, 1993) and David Landreth, *The Face of Mammon: The Matter of Money in English Renaissance Literature* (Oxford: Oxford University Press, 2012).

22 Gregory Kneidel, "Coscus, Queen Elizabeth, and Law in John Donne's *Satyre II*," *Renaissance Quarterly* 61 (2009):92–121 (104–5).

23 Eileen Spring, *Law, Land, and Family: Aristocratic Inheritance in England, 1300–1800* (Chapel Hill, NC: University of North Carolina Press, 1993), pp. 35–6, 72.

24 The differences in inheritance practices among different status groups are discussed in several of the essays in Jack Goody, Joan Thirsk, and E. P. Thompson, eds., *Family and Inheritance in Western Europe 1200–1800* (Cambridge: Cambridge University Press, 1978). Though in this book I will not have reason to attend to them, there are also significant differences regionally from one part of England to another, some of them enshrined in law (such as Kent's "gavelkind" or partible inheritance) but many of them not.

25 Quoted in Ilia Gurlyand, "Reminiscences of A. P. Chekhov," *Teatr i iskusstvo* (11 July 1904), p. 521.

26 Douglas Bruster examines an aspect of this variation, the different number and kinds of small objects or hand props used onstage in different dramatic genres, in "The Dramatic Life of Objects in Early Modern Theater," chapter 4 in *Shakespeare and the Question of Culture* (New York: Palgrave Macmillan, 2003), pp. 95–118.

27 See, for instance, the discussion of Richard II as an "unripe Hamlet" in W. B. Yeats's "At Stratford-on-Avon, Part II," originally published May 18, 1901; also the comments in C. F. Tucker Brooke's *The Tudor Drama: A History of English National Drama to the Retirement of Shakespeare* (1911) and Ivor B. Johns's "Introduction to *Richard II*" (1912), all reprinted in Charles R. Forker, ed., *Richard II*, Shakespeare: The Critical Tradition (London: Athlone Press, 1998).

28 The connection between title and lands is not always as tight as Bolingbroke claims it to be—aristocratic titles could, in some circumstances, be inherited by someone other than the heir to the estate in land that had originally supported that title—although such a separation was unusual and was considered highly undesirable.

29 Susan Bright and John Dewar, eds., *Land Law: Themes and Perspectives* (Oxford: Oxford University Press, 1998), pp. 15–51.

30 Carol Rose, *Property and Persuasion: Essays on the History, Theory, and Rhetoric of Ownership* (Boulder, CO: Westview Press, 1994), p. 59.

31 Morris Cohen, in the classic essay "Property and Sovereignty," *Cornell Law Quarterly* 13 (1927): 8–30, writing soon after the 1925 Law of Property Act abolished many remnants of feudal land tenure in Great Britain, lays out the political implications clearly: "Back of the complicated law of settlement, fee tail, copyhold estates, of the heir-at-law, of the postponement of women, and other feudal incidents, there was a great

and well founded fear that by simplifying and modernizing the real property law of England the land might become more marketable. Once land becomes fully marketable it can no longer be counted on to remain in the hands of the landed aristocratic families, and this means the passing of their political power and the end of their control over the destinies of the British empire.... From the point of view of an established land economy, a money economy thus seems a state of perpetual war instead of a social order where son succeeds father. The motto that a career should be open to talent thus seems a justification of anarchy, just as the election of rulers (kings or priests) seems an anarchic procedure to those used to the regular succession of father by son" (pp. 9–10). Later in the article, Cohen argues that many of the political powers of feudal landowners persist, in occluded form, in modern times among large property owners, heads of corporations, and the like.

32 Technically any felon's lands "escheated" to his overlord (that is, his rights in the land were terminated). However, in cases of high treason the termination of land rights was always directly to the Crown, not to a subordinate lord, and was called "forfeiture" rather than "escheat." Since the felon was sentenced to death in either case, the loss of land rights affected not him personally but his heirs. Moreover, since the vast majority of common felons had no land to give up, the penalty of confiscation fell heaviest on those convicted of high treason, who typically hailed from circles close to the monarch. Fairly often the traitor's heir was eventually reinstated in his right, but this reinstatement was entirely at the Crown's option. The effect of forfeiture was thus to interrupt a dangerously independent chain of inheritance and reassert the monarch's authority over a family manifestly inclined to challenge it.

33 For instance, see Henry Ireton's arguments for the restriction of the franchise in the 1647 Putney Debates, reprinted in David Wootton, *Divine Right and Democracy: An Anthology of Political Writing in Stuart England* (London: Hackett, 2003), pp. 285–316.

34 For a fine discussion of the political theory that informs Gaunt's warning, a discussion upon which my analysis builds, see Donna Hamilton, "The State of Law in *Richard II*," *Shakespeare Quarterly* 34 (1983): 5–17. Hamilton, correctly in my view, rejects the influential reading of *Richard II* in the second chapter of Ernst Kantorowicz, *The King's Two Bodies: A Study in Medieval Political Theology* (Princeton, NJ: Princeton University Press, 1957), which construes *Richard II* as a brief for royal absolutism. For a succinct account of the nature of the lease in late medieval and early modern England, see Jane Whittle, "Leasehold Tenure in England c.1300–c.1600: Its Form and Incidence," in Bas J.P. van Bavel and Phillipp R. Schofield, eds., *The Development of Leasehold in Northwestern Europe, c.1200–1600* (Turnhout, Belgium: Brepols, 2008), pp. 139–54. For a more detailed and technical discussion of leasehold in *Richard II*

than I provide here, see William O. Scott, "Landholding, Leasing, and Inheritance in *Richard II*," *Studies in English Literature 1500–1900* 42:2 (2002): 275–92.

35 For the Crown's regulation, in the late medieval and Tudor period, of noblemen's armed retinues, see J. P. Cooper, "Retainers in Tudor England" in *Land, Men, and Beliefs: Studies in Early Modern History* (London: Hambledon Press, 1983), pp. 78–96. The Crown needed to balance the potential threat to its power posed by such retinues, with its sporadic need to assemble, on short notice, large numbers of suitably trained and organized troops.

36 A. W. B. Simpson, *A History of the Land Law*, second edition (Oxford: Clarendon Press, 1986), p. 247.

37 Raphael Holinshed, *Chronicles of England, Scotland, and Ireland* (London J. Johnson, 1808), reprinted with an introduction by Vernon F. Snow (New York: AMS Press, 1976), ii, pp. 849, 898.

38 See, e.g., the detailed analysis by Stopford Brooke, "Purgation through Tragic Suffering in *Richard II*," originally published in 1905, collected in Forker, ed., *Richard II*.

2

Prodigal Princes: Land and Chattels in the Second Tetralogy

Henry IV Part 1 takes up the historical thread about a year after the end of *Richard II*. As the new play begins, the strife foreseen by the Bishop of Carlisle at Richard's deposition is apparently already coming to pass. Bolingbroke's former associates rise up against him, citing the injustice of removing "Richard, that sweet, lovely rose" (*1 Henry IV* 1.3.173), and join forces with Edmund Mortimer, the "next of blood" and declared heir of the childless Richard. Their revolt is crushed in *Henry IV Part 2*, but the cause revives in *Henry VI Part 1* when the last of the Mortimers, with his dying breath, passes the story of the usurped title down to his own heir, Richard Duke of York. Bolingbroke's seizure of the throne, by muddying the legitimacy of the royal succession, creates a national propensity for violent discord that stubbornly persists until the accession of Henry VII, the first Tudor king, almost a century later.

Yet these protracted struggles are quite remarkably interrupted by the short, brilliant career of Henry V, the son of Henry IV. Although his claim to the throne depends upon, and therefore is technically no better than, his father's, the younger Henry decisively arrests, indeed reverses, the kingdom's powerful centrifugal tendencies. In contrast to his predecessors and his successors, he consolidates not only the English, but the Irish, Welsh, and Scots under his banner, invades France, and by the end of *Henry V* has incorporated that realm as well into his domains. Immediately after the young king's premature death, strife breaks out once again both between England and France and among the English nobility. King Henry V is, in other words, an outlier.

What makes him an exception? In *Henry IV Part 1*, King Henry IV frets that while Harry Percy, his young enemy, displays impressive fortitude and daring, his own Harry Plantagenet, far from promising remarkable aptitude for rule, is merely following in the footsteps of his dissolute Uncle Richard. "For all the world | As thou art to this hour was Richard then," he scolds his son, "And even as I was then is Percy now" (3.2.93–4, 96). The analogy is tempting, because Richard and Prince Hal share an aptitude for rule-breaking and prodigal excess. Yet Prince Hal triumphs where Richard fails. There are some obvious reasons for this difference, and some less obvious ones. One crucial difference is that Hal's wastrel phase, unlike Richard's, comes before, not while, he possesses sovereign power: Hal, as the new King Henry V, immediately repudiates his prodigality upon his accession to the throne. Moreover, as Prince Hal informs the audience in a soliloquy at the end of *Henry IV Part 1*, Act 1 scene 2, repudiation has been part of the plan from the beginning. In his soliloquy, the Prince describes his prodigality as a strategy designed to produce an apparently miraculous *peripeteia*, creating the new king as an unprecedented object of wonder.

Yet these disparities do not entirely explain why what seem similar patterns of behavior produce such wildly different outcomes. Instead, I would look to the way Shakespeare develops the "poetry of property" in these successive plays. Prince Hal lives in a different world from Richard, a world in which prodigality can be reinvented and put to new use. Key to this reinvention, I'll argue, are property arrangements that are available in the *Henry IV* plays, but that seem denied to Richard.

As we have seen, *Richard II* is a play about what befalls a king who dares to violate his subjects' strongly held convictions about rights in land. The microcosm of the realm is the garden of Act 3 scene 4, in which the gardeners labor to "keep law and form and due proportion" (3.4.42): pruning the hedges, rooting out the weeds, binding up the apricots in a small walled space explicitly analogized to Richard's island realm. "Superfluous branches | We lop away, that bearing boughs may live," declares the gardener (64–5), who compares this violence to that of an executioner who salvages the peace of the kingdom by "cutting off" over-lofty subjects. Over time, the properly tended garden replenishes itself by growing new shoots that are made to reproduce the form and function of the old ones; if they fail to conform, they are cut or bent to shape. Substantive renewal is not at odds with the maintenance of the status quo. On the contrary, productivity requires that new growth be guided, forcibly if necessary, into reproducing a pre-existent pattern as closely as possible. Tending the garden means managing change so as to minimize its effects.

The gardeners' activities recall not merely the protocols of wise rule, to which they are explicitly made analogous, but also the inheritance practices upon which wise rule apparently depends. Land endures perpetually and remains, in an agrarian society, not merely a form of wealth but, if cared for properly, an ongoing source of wealth. Yet while acreage persists, individual proprietors are born and die. Thus land law must address how legitimately to insert a succession of persons into a proprietary role. Generally, once a vassal received a grant of land from a feudal superior, the legal mechanism of entailment, bolstered by custom, restricted the descent of the estate to "heirs of the body" or "heirs male of the body." It was sometimes possible to override this mechanism—to "break the entailment"—but the process required the expert use of a collusive legal fiction, and involved considerable expense. The impediments to selling one's "fee" or feudal land grant, or bequeathing it to someone other than the designated heir, have led some writers to argue that medieval and early modern land tenure therefore isn't "ownership" as the post-feudal world considers it.

In other words, land law prescribes the same principle of minimal alteration that governs the behavior of the gardeners, who do not revamp their garden, but train the young shoot into the place previously occupied by the dead branch they have just pruned away. The heir is the person most closely akin to the previous proprietor—ideally, his eldest son, best suited to fill his empty place or to "stand in the shoes of his ancestor," as medieval and early modern lawyers phrased it. The son, inheriting from the father, is imagined to be his replica, simply displaced one generation. We see this set of assumptions operating in *Richard II* when, after Gaunt's death, York pleads with Richard to respect Bolingbroke's inherited claim upon the Duchy of Lancaster:

> Take Hereford's rights away, and take from Time
> His charters and his customary rights:

Let not tomorrow then ensue today;
Be not thyself, for how art thou a king
But by fair sequence and succession?

(2.1.196–200)

For York, tomorrow is supposed to "ensue" in a "fair sequence": "fair" in the sense both of "beautiful" and of "just." It is "fair" to the extent that its universally acceptable principles of substitution render tomorrow as much like today, and yesterday, as possible. A system of customary rights in land testifies to the enduring power of the past in the present and into the future, enforcing the socially crucial connections between subject and prince and between father and son. Customary rights both secure the stable identity of individuals and families through time—assuring that they remain "themselves"—and knit those individuals and families together into a social fabric with their feudal superiors and inferiors.

For York, customary rights are equivalent to the principle of intelligibility itself. And he has a point, for predictability is one of the main benefits of property rights: the utilitarian philosopher Jeremy Bentham, for instance, argues that such rights are best understood as a kind of expectation.[1] Yet in *Richard II*, predictability comes at a price, because the ways in which wealth can legitimately change hands are extremely constrained.[2] The *only* respectable way of acquiring title to property, it seems, is via inheritance. In actuality, the undesirable rigidity of the system produced a variety of workarounds, including the increasingly widespread use of leases, the breaking of entailments via elaborate legal fictions, and the setting up of various kinds of trust arrangements. Yet these devices, however ubiquitous and expedient, nonetheless violate an ideal of what both sovereignty and proprietary rights are supposed to entail; thus in *Richard II* the old-fashioned moralist John of Gaunt, as we have seen, considers the lease a dangerous corruption.

By the end of *Richard II*, the smooth progression from ancestor to heir has been decisively ruptured, first by Richard's actions then by Henry's, precipitating the crisis of which York warns. What can happen in a world in which it is unclear how tomorrow will succeed today—in which, in other words, the future is entirely unpredictable? As Lars Engle remarks, "Henry IV is a national parricide whose paternity to the state must therefore always be in question and whose bequest to his son must necessarily be troubled."[3] How can Prince Hal "stand in the shoes of his ancestor" without simply repeating his father's crimes?

Although the events of *Henry IV Part 1* follow almost immediately upon those at the end of *Richard II*, the world of the play, as many critics have noted, is radically different. What actually ensues is not a miraculous restoration of the past, but a different arrangement in which new socio-proprietary possibilities unexpectedly flower. These possibilities, I shall argue, are founded not upon land but upon chattels—moveable property.

The new prominence and prestige of the chattel in the *Henry IV* plays is remarkable. In *Richard II*, after Richard has been formally deposed, he asks leave to depart, and Bolingbroke obliges him: "Go, some of you, convey him to the Tower." To which Richard bitterly responds, "O good, 'convey!' Conveyors are you all, | That rise thus nimbly by a true king's fall" (4.1.306–8). He plays on two senses of the word "convey," one meaning simply "transport," the other meaning "steal." The pun brings out what all the characters in *Richard II* seem to believe, that "conveyance" is always illegitimate: property is supposed to "descend" from father to son in a prescribed line of inheritance, not to move laterally or to "convey." In *Richard II* Richard's appropriation of Bolingbroke's inheritance is wrong, and so, of course, is Bolingbroke's appropriation of Richard's.

The world of the *Henry IV* plays, by contrast, is a world on the move, dominated by "conveyance" in all its senses. While in *Richard II* the realm is metonymized as a walled, aggressively cultivated garden, *Henry IV Part 1* sets a similarly memorable vignette in the stables attached to a bustling roadside inn at Rochester, on the road traversed in one direction by "pilgrims going to Canterbury with rich offerings," and in the other direction by "traders riding to London with fat purses." Alan Stewart has recently discussed the importance to the play of the "carriers" featured in this scene, who make their living transporting people and goods from one location to another.[4] Carriers are the avatars of the chattel economy.

In medieval and early modern English common law there are dramatic differences (which in the centuries since have nearly vanished) between the rules governing property in chattels and those governing property in land. The complex forms of tenure have no relevance to chattel property, nor does entailment; chattels can normally be bequeathed simply at the will of a testator. These differences flow out of material differences between land and chattels, differences which pose contrasting practical dilemmas for property holders. As we have seen, a landholding society must confront the fact that its property is going to persist beyond the lifetime of individual proprietors, so that some means must be arranged to transfer that property to successors in an orderly way. The other practical problem posed by land is that it is immoveable. A feudal or semi-feudal system overcomes these apparent disadvantages by linking land intimately to the exercise of power and investing that power in noble bloodlines tied to particular locales. Chattel property poses a different range of challenges. As the English term for them indicates, chattels are "moveable": property rights in chattels need to specify which kinds of movement are legitimate and which are not. Their portability is intimately linked with their other difference from land, their relative impermanence: chattels can be lost, stolen, irrecoverably damaged, or obliterated. This difference is, in many cases, only a relative one, for a good deal of early modern chattel property was extremely sturdy: furniture, cooking pots, mattresses, and other household goods were manufactured to last for generations, so that their value hardly depreciated over the course of a single lifetime.[5] Yet the issue of durability does arise urgently in the class of chattels classified as "consumable," in other words, goods that are annihilated in the course of use, like stores of food and drink. "The turkeys in my pannier are half-starved," announces one carrier as he prepares to hurry to London: their deaths are pending, either from their own hunger or because they will soon be slaughtered to feed their urban purchasers. The prominence of consumables in the *Henry IV* plays— sack, bread, ale, bacon, and so on—has the effect of making the distinction between land and chattels seem particularly emphatic; to define them, for the plays' purposes, as conceptual opposites.

"Consumables" are also the form of property with which the prodigal is particularly associated. The prodigal story originates, of course, in the gospel of Luke, and has a long history of adaptation and interpretation in the Christian tradition. It is probably most often understood on an individual level: God the Father remains open to a sinner's repentance, and will always welcome him home. However, the Geneva Bible, following a common patristic interpretation, glosses the parable as a story about nations: the elder brother, who remains with the father, stands for the Jews, and the younger brother, at first lost to God but eventually reconciled, for the Gentiles. Modern critics of English Renaissance literature emphasize the ambivalent drama of generational transition. For instance, Richard Helgerson argues that the cohort of writers who came of age in the 1580s and 1590s understood themselves as "prodigals": shut out of the opportunities for advancement that had been plentiful for educated men in the 1550s and 1560s, they were beset by convictions of inadequacy and shameful deviation from the paternal example.[6]

Yet the parable of the prodigal son is a story about property, too. The restless young man takes his portion, journeys into a far country, and there squanders it in loose living. Luke does not explicitly indicate the form in which the family of origin holds its wealth, but details of the parable suggest a prosperous farm: a vineyard, well-fed servants, an elder brother toiling in the field, a fatted calf killed upon the return of the penitent. In order to extract his share of the inheritance and take it into a foreign land, the prodigal son must therefore convert his patrimony into chattel property, "movables" capable of being taken away.

In the parable, the prodigal son's exchange of permanent, stable land for transient goods is disastrously imprudent, and he ends up a bankrupt. In late Elizabethan and Jacobean England, the situation of the prodigal had an obvious contemporary application: conspicuous consumption among elites soared even as inflation eroded real income from land rents, and strapped noblemen and gentry made up the difference by mortgaging or selling their land.[7] In many early modern satiric treatments, as in the story in the Bible, prodigal behavior seems wickedly foolish, while the father represents the good alternative: forbearing, sustaining, forgiving, and perhaps most importantly, predictably remaining in the fruitful home where he belongs, rather than squandering his all in a foreign place. At least superficially, *Richard II* seems wholly to endorse this profoundly conservative view. The fathers Edward III and the Black Prince established a pattern of prudent property management, and of military and sexual effectiveness, which their delinquent heir fails to emulate. And he suffers for it.

The *Henry IV* plays, however, pair the revaluing of the prodigal with a partial revaluing of the consumable commodity. "Movables," as all the urban scenes demonstrate, are easily deracinated and rearranged out of context. The Eastcheap tavern, especially, is a place of objects cut loose, consumable odds and ends, many of them apparently diverted from their "proper" owners. Falstaff's pockets, emptied, yield a tavern reckoning, a list of things that have already, of course, ceased to exist: "Item: a capon...Item: sauce...Item: sack, two gallons...Item: anchovies and sack after supper...Item: bread" (*1 Henry IV* 2.5.488–92). It is easy to see, in these moments, why a society that values stability, predictability, and easily discerned order would find chattel property less significant than land, and might be inclined not to see consumable chattels as a form of "wealth" at all. Yet the transience of such consumables has a powerful positive valence as well. Because they are not inherited from forebears but selected and purchased by the consumer, they can therefore function as markers of individual style. In fact the more ephemeral the goods, and the more frequent such purchases must therefore be, the stronger their personal expressiveness. In *Henry IV Part 1,* Falstaff's capon, sack, and morsel of bread thus testify vividly to his own intemperate nature, not—as a landed inheritance would do—to his family origins.

An alternative name for chattel property in early modern common law, "personalty," implies the connection between the object and its owner considered as an individual with particular accoutrements and tastes. Because, as we have seen, chattel property can be purchased on a whim and given away or bequeathed as its owner dictates, it is closely associated with personal idiosyncrasy and with affiliations that do not necessarily dovetail with the genealogical presumptions of intimacy enshrined in land law. Thus historians often focus on wills because these documents provide evidence for relationships that fall outside dynastic imperatives: intimate friendships between women, for instance.[8] In Shakespeare's own will, his chattel bequests, most notoriously his bestowal of the "second best bed" upon his wife, have attracted the attention of biographers because, as the points at which he might have decided differently, these stipulations seem to offer fleeting insight into his character. In other words, both land and chattels are "connected" to their owners, but the form of the connection—what the property "says" about the proprietor—is fundamentally different in the two cases. Insofar as chattels express and respond to the appetites, pleasures, and choices of individuals, they are imagined—in Shakespeare's Eastcheap, in Middleton's Cheapside, in Jonson's Bartholomew Fair—not in terms of a rational fitting of demand to supply, but as luxurious self-indulgence inevitably tending to waste and excess. While the rules of land tenure seem designed to ensure permanence by offsetting the mortality of individuals, the relatively unregulated chattel emphasizes the prospect of death and mutability.

From a conservative, feudal point of view, the relationships associated with chattels, established on grounds other than blood relationship or the need for dynastic perpetuation, might seem aimless or even dangerous. The mechanism of inheritance links land, imagined as permanent and self-renewing, to a dynasty hoped to be similarly permanent and self-renewing. The family tree roots itself in the soil of the family estate.[9] The prodigal's heedless conversion of land wealth into expendable chattel wealth therefore has a social equivalent, a preference for unrelated acquaintances over kinfolk, and a sexual equivalent, a preference for pleasure over procreation. In the parable of the prodigal son, the younger brother wastes his patrimony "among companions," and the resentful elder brother complains to his father that his younger brother has "devoured thy goods with harlots." In *Richard II*, Richard's critics likewise connect the king's property transgressions to his enjoyment of women pandered by Bushy, Bagot, and Green—or perhaps his enjoyment of Bushy, Bagot, and Green themselves. It doesn't matter what the precise sexual transgressions are, only that, in Bolingbroke's words, Richard's companions "Made a divorce betwixt his queen and him, | Broke the possession of a royal bed" (3.1.13) and therefore precluded the generation of an heir. The place of transgression is likewise significant. Renaissance depictions of the prodigal son in his riotous phase generally show him with fellow male revelers, his "companions," disporting themselves in a whorehouse. The brothel, inn, or tavern, in the prodigal son story and in the *Henry IV* plays, is the commodified double of a repudiated domesticity, selling to transients what they "ought to" get at home for free.

In *Richard II*, Richard's contempt for kinship bonds—his preference for "upstarts" over his own uncles and cousins—seems impossibly presumptuous and indeed eventually proves suicidal. Yet in *Henry IV*, voluntary affiliations flourish. Prince Hal enjoys the society of Falstaff, Poins, and Mistress Quickly even while the King scolds his son: "thy affections...hold a wing | Quite from the flight of all thy ancestors" (*1 Henry IV*, 3.2.30–1). The oft-remarked "queerness" of the association between Hal and Falstaff lies, I think, not so much in the homosexuality some critics have detected,[10] as more simply in its whimsically elective quality, which seems to defy the dynastic logic that dominates so many of Shakespeare's histories. And yet in the busy, various world of the *Henry IV* plays, political leadership requires the ruler not only to manage the disputes and jockeying for power among his fractious extended family, as Richard II failed to do, but also—even mainly— to inspire and lead people who are not his kin. The ruler must learn to cultivate those non-familial, elective or expedient relationships with which chattel property is conceptually aligned.

In the *Henry IV* plays, moreover, chattel exchanges achieve a new imaginative importance in social spheres apparently far removed from the gritty world of the carriers and their turkeys and gammons of bacon. Whereas, in Shakespeare's England, it was routine to oppose the "honor" of aristocratic chivalry to the "base" dealings of the commercial world, the *Henry IV* plays provocatively imagine chivalrous warfare as transactions involving moveable property. Early in *Henry IV Part 1*, the question of Mortimer's, or Hotspur's, valor in battle almost immediately gives way to a quarrel over who has the right to take, and the obligation to pay, ransom for prisoners. War is a profit-making activity, a merchandising of valuable captives. Later, in conversation with his father, Prince Hal memorably imagines himself as a business principal who has sent an agent abroad to transact on his behalf. He tells King Henry:

> Percy is but my factor, good my lord,
> To engross up glorious deeds on my behalf;
> And I will call him to so strict account
> That he shall render every glory up...

> (3.2.147–50)

Whereas in the parable of the prodigal son the young man runs off to foreign parts and squanders his goods, in *Henry IV Part 1* the young voyager, Hotspur, "engrosses," or accumulates at wholesale rates, "glorious deeds" that he will need to relinquish to his superior upon his return. The poetics of property in chattels redefines both errancy and homecoming: instead of a wastrel, a merchant-adventurer; instead of a welcoming father at the end of the long circular journey, a corporate superior legitimately appropriating and profiting from the efforts of his delegate.

Thus Prince Hal's own prodigality is a new phenomenon, in keeping with the newly flexible and varied economic realities of his environment, an environment that gives him resources unavailable to his uncle Richard. Whereas the traditional prodigal story contrasts the reckless dispersal of chattel wealth "abroad" with the prudent management of land wealth "at home," in a commercial economy the mobility of persons and goods no longer inevitably entails ruin. Indeed, the shrewd management of chattels may now become a potential source of wealth in its own right.

Prince Hal makes prodigality, or what looks like it, a form of prudence: so offending, as he says, to make offense a skill. This skill requires sensitivity to new variables and the cultivation of a different set of ethical priorities. While in *Richard II* rigid rules of primogeniture determined the legitimacy of any change in proprietary rights, so that fungibility was limited or non-existent, a chattel transaction involves an exchange: a buyer typically wants not the same things he laid out to be returned to him, but other things. In the *Henry IV* plays the emphasis on traffic in chattels legitimizes various forms of substitution, giving the Prince considerable latitude. Yet that doesn't mean that anything goes. In a chattel economy, the primary criterion of justice is whether transactions are *fair*: whether property is exchanged in proper ratios. It is no accident, then, that Prince Hal shows a punctilious attention to adequate recompense. If one takes property and does not pay for it, one is a thief—Falstaff's impenitent fleecing of the Hostess is of a piece with his robberies. If, on the other hand, one pays back what one has stolen, the plays imagine that equilibrium is restored, as if the theft had never occurred, even though in early modern as in contemporary law repayment does not cancel the criminality of the original seizure. Prince Hal shows his future kingliness by not merely paying back what he owes, but, in a royally magnanimous gesture, paying back *more* than he owes. In *Henry IV Part 1*, not only does the Prince return the money to the robbed passengers "with advantage" (2.5.498), but more generally, he anticipates eventually "paying the debt I never promised" by throwing off his "loose behavior" (1.2.186–7).[11]

Prospering in a chattel economy requires patience and a tolerance for risk. The feudal landholding idealized by Gaunt and York in *Richard II* minimizes, insofar as possible, any discrepancy between today and tomorrow, and imagines the heir gliding quietly into his father's place at exactly that point at which he attains his maturity. The father's demise is supposed to coincide with the son's coming of age, as, in the gardener's analogy, the pruning of the dead branch makes room for the sprouting one. Obscured in this fantasy of smooth transition and orderly duplication is the fact that demographic contingency makes succession ragged and unpredictable. The Black Prince perishes prematurely, leaving Richard a kingdom he is too young to rule, while Prince Hal's father remains alive and still vigorous even after his son's adulthood. While Richard is hurried into a role he is not yet capable of filling, Hal is forced to wait, with the predictable consequence that many of his associates, and even the King himself, casually assume that he is "naturally" eager for his father's death. For while the father survives, his heir dangles in limbo. If the son's coming into his full powers requires the extinction of his father, the relationship between the two of them naturally becomes fraught.

Yet Hal repudiates the "envy" of this aspersion, and he does so convincingly because he cultivates an attitude toward temporality drawn from a commercial order that not only acknowledges the difference between today and tomorrow, but attempts to profit from it. The deliberate management of temporal gaps is basic to any economy based on chattel transactions: goods are extended on credit, and the supplier only paid afterward; investors lay out money in hopes of a future return. The harnessing of temporal heterogeneity—the difference between tomorrow and today—is basic as well to Hal's shrewd exploitation of the otherwise "empty" time before he comes to the throne. He channels the time-consciousness required for the effective deployment of chattel wealth into a drama of

performed errancy and final reconciliation with the father, a drama
the success of which becomes clear only in retrospect. In the biblical
parable, the prodigal son's squandering is a *felix culpa*, a fortunate
fall that leads to repentance and redemption, but the felicity is only
visible at the end of the story. Viewed at an earlier point, say when
the boy was yearning hungrily for the husks fed to the swine, it looks
as unhappy as any fall, as unprofitable as an extension of credit or
an investment of capital would look if it were evaluated before the
return were factored in. What the Prince calls "redeeming time" is
not, therefore, merely a matter of using time wisely, but of revealing,
after the fact, that an unsuspected profit has accrued: an educational
benefit, a propaganda coup. "Redemption" here is both a religious
and a fiscal concept, linking spiritual renewal with a surprising, because belated, financial return.

The King, of course, worries that Prince Hal is simply repeating
Richard's mistakes. Despite his own gross disruption of the inheritance system, Henry IV is conceptually shackled to its norms. He
sees the current generation as a replica of the last one, and can only
understand his son as a copy of a past type, albeit unaccountably
deriving from a collateral line—from the uncle. Critics who disap-
prove of the "mercantile" world of the Henry plays and in particular
of the Prince's participation in this world sometimes seem to share
the King's attitude. Robert Ornstein, for instance, deplores the
Prince's cognizance of what kinds of exchanges and substitutions
are permissible, his reckoning of what risks it is appropriate to take
in pursuit of a self-interested profit, his awareness that delaying dis-
closure of one's wares may whet desire for them.

> Hal's diction and metaphors associate his calculated redemp-
> tion with the crassness of commodity and sharp business prac-
> tices...Like a clever Elizabethan shopkeeper, Hal knows how
> to display the merchandise of his behavior in such a light that
> it appears richer than it is.[12]

To Ornstein, to be "calculating" is perforce to be morally suspect
and déclassé. This criticism, like King Henry's, seems premised
upon a John of Gaunt-like nostalgia for feudal simplicity, and upon
the conviction that the calculations of commerce are incompatible
with an aristocratic ethos. The *Henry IV* plays emphatically suggest

otherwise, and yet they do not entirely preclude a dystopic view of the competitiveness and struggle for advantage entailed by quasi-commercial enterprise. "No one in the play is innocent," as Jonathan Goldberg remarks; "predation is endemic."[13]

Two factors complicate the "rise of the chattel" in the *Henry IV* plays. The first is that the primary issue of contention remains land: a civil war is, after all, being fought over the control of territory. Chattel transactions coexist with land tenure in a complex amalgam, just as they did in Shakespeare's world. One effect of that amalgam is that what land means in the *Henry IV* plays is no longer exactly the same as what it meant in *Richard II*. In *Richard II* the realm is imagined as indivisible, a single jewel "set in a silver sea," upon which sovereignty is uniquely and literally "grounded," and which is either possessed completely or entirely lost. In the *Henry IV* plays, by contrast, land is sometimes imagined as something trans-acted for, bargained over, and divided up. The rebels, haggling over a map of the British Isles, no longer romanticize the unity of the realm; and Hotspur does not even respect internal natural bounda-ries, offering instead to manipulate them by rechanneling the River Trent. Nonetheless, land still retains its connection to political power and remains tied to a rigid system of transfer via inheritance.

Indeed, the Prince's strategy would be impossible were the rules of land tenure and the transfer of title less secure than they actually are. In Shakespeare's time, it was widely recognized that the rule of primogeniture encouraged presumptuous behavior on the part of the heir apparent, insofar as it tied his father's hands. Chief Justice Popham observes in 1594 that an irrevocably guaranteed inherit-ance encourages "disobedience in children to their parents, when they see that they shall have their patrimony against their will, whereby such children often times become unnatural and disso-lute."[14] For Popham, this is reason enough for loosening the strait-jacket of the primogenital system. Yet King Henry's own flagrant disregard for the rule of primogeniture in his overthrow of Richard has made it all the more critical that he observe that rule now, to establish the legitimacy of his own dynasty. The King might wish it could be proven that some fairy had exchanged his Harry for Harry Percy in their cradles, but absent such proof, the Prince need not fear that his father might attempt to bequeath the kingdom to

Hotspur or even to his younger brother, John of Lancaster. Because, king or no king, Henry IV cannot alter the succession to accord with his personal preferences. If, on the other hand, in order to become king the Prince needed to ingratiate himself with his father, demonstrating from the outset his superiority to rival claimants, then he would not be able to afford a strategy that becomes comprehensible as a strategy only after his father's demise. He has the luxury of biding his time, knowing he can offer himself as his father's duplicate at the appropriate moment. "Not Amurath an Amurath succeeds," he reassures his brothers after his father's death, "but Harry Harry" (*2 Henry IV*, 5.2.48–9). Not only does ironclad primogeniture install him in his right, a Harry succeeding a Harry, but it protects his siblings, because their clear *lack* of right prevents the flare-up of dangerous rivalry. Unlike "Amurath" or Murad II, the Turkish sultan who upon his accession had his five younger brothers strangled, the new Henry V extends quasi-paternal care for his siblings and receives their support in return. "I'll be your father and your brother too | Let me but bear your love, I'll bear your cares" (*2 Henry IV*, 5.2.57). At the end of the two plays, the heir stands in the shoes of his ancestor after all.

Another complicating factor, limiting the way in which chattel transactions might provide a model for kingly conduct in either of the *Henry IV* plays, is that history maps only very imperfectly upon the simple chattel exchange. In a chattel transaction the moment of reckoning occurs when payment is received or when the investment pays off, and the principals can accurately calculate their gains or losses. Likewise in the parable of the prodigal son, as we have seen, the young man's homecoming is the point at which the story's meaning resolves and a moral can be drawn. Prince Hal's early career, like the time-sensitive mercantile bargain, can only be assessed for its profitability in retrospect, yet Shakespeare's history plays leave pointedly unclear when is the appropriate occasion for retrospection and assessment. The battle of Shrewsbury? The accession of Prince Hal as King Henry V? The conquest of France? The civil strife that follows Henry V's death, foretold at the deposition of Richard II by the Bishop of Carlisle and again by the Chorus immediately after the triumphant conclusion to *Henry V*? The ambiguities and ironies of Shakespeare's history cycle highlight the ways in which apparently climactic moments, when an appraisal finally seems possible, turn out not to be so definitive as they appear.

At issue, here, of course, is not merely a distinction between chattels and land but a discontinuity between "literary form", which has an end, and history, which does not. And this is not the only issue on which literature and life diverge. The parable of the prodigal son, like many Bible stories and folk tales, reverses the priorities of common law and the rules of succession, not to mention what might seem elementary fairness, by surprisingly preferring the wild younger son over his dutiful elder brother. In other words, while "real life," with its constraints upon inheritance and its tight connection between land and power, favors the elder, the world of stories favors the younger; indeed the counterfactuality is essential for the story's element of surprise and delight. In plays that are themselves hybrid, Prince Hal, with one foot in the "historical" world of the Shrewsbury battlefield and the other in the "fictional" world of the Eastcheap tavern, combines the real-life advantages of the elder son with the literary advantages of the younger son, just as he strategically employs both the rules of the chattel economy and the conventions of land tenure to his advantage.

Prince Hal also combines what are, in the parable of the prodigal son, the distinct roles of the father and the son. In the parable, the son's redemption is the free gift of the forgiving father, who receives the repentant youth as his child, not as a slave. Moreover, the father's resources are implied to be infinite: that is why the elder brother is mistaken to grumble over the munificent welcome of the younger brother, because the wealth dedicated to the younger does not apparently detract from the wealth afforded to the elder. Over the course of the *Henry IV* plays, by contrast, Prince Hal engineers both his "fall" and his "redemption," finally declaring himself reformed at the moment of his accession to the throne as his father's heir. In so doing he elides what in the parable is the salvific role of the father, or rather he plays both roles himself, as he and Falstaff do in jest at the Boar's Head Tavern. No wonder King Henry feels sidelined and slighted.

In short, Hal apparently gets it all: the advantages of land and the advantages of chattels, the advantages of being an elder son and the advantages of being a younger son, the advantages of being a father and the advantages of being the father's heir. The effect is to redefine and relocate the plenitude that, in the old system, was identified with the father and with patrimonial landholding. Now plenty and success become, like chattels, personal choices and characteristics: in other word, *functions of character*, imagined as ineffable, non-transferable properties of a particular individual. In *Inalienable Possessions*, the anthropologist Annette Weiner points out that the powerful chieftain is not, as Marcel Mauss had imagined in his work on the primitive gift, the one who actually gives away all his substance without regard to the morrow; rather it is he who successfully deploys what Weiner calls the art of "keeping-while-giving," *seeming* to give everything away even while he cunningly reserves wealth for himself that he never alienates. In Weiner's account, lavish generosity, apparent squandering, is not the alternative to, but the expression of, a successful economic calculation.[15] The powerful chieftain can afford to be bountiful because he manages his resources well, and his extreme liberality is all the more intimidating insofar as the recipients of his gifts know that he is not actually bankrupting himself. In a rather similar way Hal can turn the prodigal story back upon itself because, in fact, he is not bound by its cautionary tale of the danger of waste.

The fact that he is not so bound strikes his contemporaries, subjects, and even enemies as miraculous. "I saw young Harry with his beaver on," reports Vernon,

> His cuishes on his thighs, gallantly armed,
> Rise from the ground like feathered Mercury,
> And vaulted with such ease into his seat
> As if an angel dropped down from the clouds
> To turn and wind a fiery Pegasus,
> And witch the world with noble horsemanship.

> (4.1.105–11)

Hal's superhumanly gifted horsemanship is all the more astonishing because, as far as anyone can tell, he has spent his days carousing rather than training as a warrior. Just as in *Richard II*, horsemanship is a distinctly aristocratic accomplishment metaphorically aligned with self-control and with the ability to rule, and Hal apparently possesses it innately, without instruction or practice, as a form of "nobility" unrelated to the apparently contingent domain of property relations. Like other forms of *sprezzatura*, the Prince's prodigality involves a withholding of resources ironically calculated to create an appearance of lavish expenditure.

"I shall hereafter, my thrice-gracious lord, | be more myself," the Prince promises his father (*1 Henry IV*, 3.2,92–3). The investment in the personality of the prince can easily be deconstructed as a mystification. But it is a mystification with which the *Henry IV* plays, and most of *Henry V*, seem almost entirely complicit. Only in the epilogue to *Henry V* do the serious disadvantages of the protagonist's strategies of kingship fully emerge. Ruling by force of character, Henry V engineers a triumph of national amalgamation which is essentially personal rather than institutional. Its personal quality is demonstrated by its abrupt and immediate collapse in the absence of the strong force that holds it together. The King, described by the Prologue to *Henry V* as "warlike Harry, like himself," cannot, in fact, *reproduce* what the plays suggest is a non-replicable individual excellence. If the "ancestor" is *sui generis*, then there is no way his descendant can possibly "stand in his shoes." The only kingly function that King Henry V fails to execute triumphantly is, therefore, to "compound," with his French princess Katherine, "a boy...that shall go to Constantinople and take the Turk by the beard" (*Henry V*, 5.2.195–6). Like "Alexander the Pig," to whom Fluellen compares him, Henry V is a prodigy whose glorious accomplishments evaporate soon after his demise. Possibly the bleak consequences of dynastic failure may have been weighing on the minds of Shakespeare and his contemporaries, toward the close of the Virgin Queen's long and remarkable reign. At any rate in King Henry's case, his failure seems dictated by the nature of his success.

Notes

1 Jeremy Bentham, *The Theory of Legislation*, trans. and ed. Charles Milner Atkinson from the French of Etienne Dumont (Oxford: Oxford University Press, 1914), pp. 145–7.

2 In addition to inheritance it is acceptable, even admirable, for monarchs—but only monarchs—to gain territory by foreign conquest: an exception that matters little in *Richard II*, but that will become important

in *Henry V*. There are practical connections between inheritance and conquest in the feudal land tenure system, in which land originally was granted in return for military service, and to enable vassals to support the horses and armed men they were required to supply their lord in time of need. In *Richard II*, Gaunt and York imagine conquest, like inheritance, as reinforcing the connection between father and son: the Black Prince emulates his own father, King Edward III, in conquering French territory.

3 Lars Engle, *Shakespearean Pragmatism: Market of His Time* (Chicago, IL: University of Chicago Press, 1993), p. 115.

4 Alan Stewart, "Shakespeare and the Carriers," in *Shakespeare's Letters* (Oxford: Oxford University Press, 2008), pp. 115–54.

5 Amy Louise Erickson, *Women and Property in Early Modern England* (New York: Routledge, 1993), p. 66.

6 Richard Helgerson, *The Elizabethan Prodigals* (Berkeley, CA: University of California Press, 1976).

7 The classic description of the financial bind of the landowning classes is Lawrence Stone's *Crisis of the Aristocracy, 1558–1641* (Oxford: Oxford University Press, 1965).

8 See e.g. the analyses in Jack Goody, Joan Thirsk, and E. P. Thompson, eds., *Family and Inheritance in Western Europe 1200–1800* (Cambridge: Cambridge University Press, 1978); Erickson, *Women and Property in Early Modern England*; and Alan Bray, *The Friend* (Chicago, IL: University of Chicago Press, 2003).

9 For an analysis of the way the "family tree" is imagined to be rooted in "family ground" on the national as well as clan level, see Jean Feerick, "'Divided by soyle': Plantation and Degeneracy in *The Tempest* and *The Sea Voyage*," *Renaissance Drama* 35 (2006): 27–54.

10 For discussions of the play's homoerotics, see e.g. Heather Findlay, "Renaissance Pederasty and Pedagogy: the 'Case' of Shakespeare's Falstaff," *Yale Journal of Criticism* 3 (1989): 229–38 and Jonathan Goldberg, "Desiring Hal," in *Sodometries: Renaissance Texts, Modern Sexualities* (Stanford, CA: Stanford University Press, 1992), pp. 145–75.

11 E. Rubinstein, "*1 Henry IV*: The Metaphor of Liability," *Studies in English Literature 1500–1900* 10 (1970): 287–95.

12 Robert Ornstein, *A Kingdom for A Stage: The Achievement of Shakespeare's History Plays* (Cambridge, MA: Harvard University Press, 1972), pp. 137–8.

13 Jonathan Goldberg, *Sodometries: Renaissance Texts, Modern Sexualities* (Stanford, CA: Stanford University Press, 1992), p. 153.

14 Sir John Popham, *Reports and Cases,* second edition (London: John Place, 1682), p. 80. Popham offers this remark in the course of his report on Dillon v. Fraine, otherwise known as Chudleigh's Case, one of the most important land law cases of the period.

15 Annette Weiner, *Inalienable Possessions: The Paradox of Keeping-While-Giving* (Berkeley, CA: University of California Press, 1992), pp. 23–65, 149–55.

3

Heirs and Affines in *The Merchant of Venice*

In the past two chapters, I have argued that between *Richard II* and the *Henry IV* plays we move from a world dominated by landed inheritance to a more flexible and varied economy that includes chattel transactions. Since at least the nineteenth century, it has been common to read Shakespeare's second tetralogy as a meditation upon the decline of feudalism,[1] and perhaps my analysis might be seen as extending that tradition, emphasizing the change in property arrangements in the late medieval and early modern period. This reading of the second tetralogy generally posits that Shakespeare settled the theme of the four plays from the outset. Yet perhaps instead, something intervened between the writing of *Richard II* and the writing of *Henry IV Part 1* that encouraged Shakespeare to reimagine the problems of property and personhood. The dating of Shakespeare's plays is a murky and contested issue, but many scholars and editors have argued that *The Merchant of Venice* was written between *Richard II* (1595) and the *Henry IV* plays (1597–9).[2] If so, it previews some of the concerns of the latter plays: the question of one's responsibility for one's debts, the nature of children's obligation to parents and vice versa, and the connection between prodigality and commercial venturing. Prince Hal's image of Hotspur as a "factor," venturing abroad to gather honor on Hal's behalf, assimilates the Prince to men like Antonio in *The Merchant of Venice*, sedentary merchants whose vessels ply trading routes to Mexico, the Indies, England, and north Africa.

In fact, *The Merchant of Venice* is more exclusively and obsessively concerned with the nexus between a character and his possessions than the plays I have yet examined. Such critics as Marc Shell, Lars Engle, and David Landreth have described the play's concern with what Shell calls "the apparent commensurability (even identity) of men and money."[3] The romantic hero Bassanio's motives for wooing Portia seem bluntly pecuniary: she is "a lady richly left," and he hopes to repay his debts to Antonio from her inheritance. While plenty of romantic heroines defy their fathers, the staging of Jessica's elopement foregrounds her theft of paternal property. She tosses a casket to Lorenzo, then "gilds" herself with "mo ducats" before departing; later she is reported to have stolen two jewels from Shylock, spent eighty ducats in a night, and exchanged a turquoise ring for a monkey. The Christians ridicule Shylock for equating "my ducats and my daughter," and yet the play often seems to do exactly that.

Yet the equation is never complete or untroubled. Again and again in *The Merchant of Venice* we see both the way the two terms can be conflated, and the impulse to distinguish between them. When Antonio offers "purse and person" to Bassanio, or Bassanio acknowledges that he owes Antonio "the most in money and in love," they simultaneously suggest a parallel and draw a distinction between purse and person, money and love. Many other key terms in *The Merchant of Venice*—"worth," "credit," "bond," "mine," and "yours"—similarly hover uneasily between their economic signification and a sense that seems to escape or transcend economic calculation.

The obviousness of *Merchant's* concern with such matters is partly an effect of genre. While Shakespeare makes important modifications in the historical materials he receives from Holinshed and Hall, departing in especially striking ways in the *Henry IV* plays, he is still tied by the need to present more or less "what happened." In *The Merchant of Venice*, by contrast, as Harley Granville-Barker commented long ago, "There is no more reality in Shylock's bond and the Lord of Belmont's will than in Jack and the Beanstalk."[4] The play's fictions highlight the question of what can be bartered for, exchanged, contracted for, and what can't, in a way that is more pointed, because more counterfactually vivid, than the history plays can accommodate.

The Merchant of Venice often exaggerates or distorts even what seem like realistic features of the transactions it depicts. Several critics have commented upon the fact that an actual merchant of Antonio's stature would have insured himself against losses: marine insurance came into use between the twelfth and fourteenth centuries in Italian mercantile cities, and had reached England by Shakespeare's time, precisely because it spread and controlled the otherwise intolerable risks of long-distance international commerce in fragile wooden sailing ships.[5] Similarly, as I will discuss shortly in more detail, the fact that Portia is selected via a casket test is not the only way in which her union with Bassanio is out of the ordinary. On the other hand, in some respects the play scrupulously reproduces details of laws and customs concerning debt and credit. Alan Stewart demonstrates, for instance, that Shylock's understanding of the sealed bond with Antonio correlates closely with common law doctrine,[6] though such bonds, of course, did not generally specify pounds of flesh in their forfeiture clauses. In fact one of the difficulties of interpreting *The Merchant of Venice* is to know when it is appropriate to understand its strange dealings as reflecting routine practice in the period, and when Shakespeare is taking poetic liberties that make that correlation improper.

The history plays by and large concern themselves with problems of rule, so that, as we have seen, property concerns tend to collapse into questions of power relations and vice versa. In *The Merchant of Venice*, though, the relationship between *dominium* and *imperium* is of minimal importance. Although Portia's unsuccessful suitors are noblemen or royalty—princes, barons, lords, a count palatine—their positions of authority in their native lands receive no attention. Nor does "Lord Bassanio" seem to play a political role in Venice; his title merely indicates that his status qualifies him as an appropriate match for Portia. Instead *The Merchant of Venice*, like most comedies, focuses upon the forging and maintenance of intimate relationships. Three kinds of intimacy are particularly at issue, and at least potentially in competition with one another: the intimacy between marriageable or married couples, the intimacy between parent and child, and the intimacy between friends of the same sex. In all these relationships, moreover, property concerns and emotional attachment, though configured differently in the different cases, overlap in ways that are frequently untidy.

The wealthy, beautiful, and intelligent Portia is perhaps the play's most prominent example of an individual whose worth seems simultaneously calculated in material and in non-material terms. For the many Jasons that come in quest of her, her allure is not merely that she is an heiress, but that she is "richly *left*"—that is, apparently under her own control. While a woman from a prosperous family normally brought a dowry or "portion" to her marriage, her bridegroom was expected to possess at least equivalent wealth and social standing. Affluent families normally enforced this rule by preventing poor fortune-hunters from gaining access to their young kinswomen. An enduring fantasy, therefore, for men of few means in early modern England was the heiress or, more commonly, rich widow who might lack (or be able to escape) the hovering solicitude of her family for her financial welfare. In George Chapman's *The Widow's Tears*, for instance, a well-to-do widow dispenses with the property requirement for bridegrooms because she is sexually captivated by her mate, an impecunious but boldly virile younger brother. In *Twelfth Night*, Malvolio is encouraged to believe that the unsupervised Olivia will behave in a similarly impetuous fashion (and she does, though she chooses Sebastian). Once again we see both the intrinsic connection between wealth and lovability and their separation: while the heiress is desirable at least in part because she is rich, the penniless suitor can sometimes gain her favor despite his lack of material resources. And once again, as in the prodigal son story, where the younger son is favored over his elder brother, we see a fiction structuring itself not as an imitation of ordinary life but as a departure from it. Whereas real-life heiresses were closely monitored, the heiress in the world of romance is at liberty to favor a poor man's enterprise, good looks, or quick wit.

Of course, Portia is not as free as she appears, as she complains to Nerissa: "I may neither choose who I would nor refuse who I dislike; so is the will of a living daughter curbed by the will of a dead father" (1.2.19–22). The casket test abrogates the usual property test for bridegrooms, but the abrogation is not, as it usually is, the reckless act of a flighty, sex-crazed, or naively unmaterialistic heiress. Rather, the test is imposed by the bride's father, and binds Portia as well as the men who try to win her. So, like most early modern heiresses, Portia must submit to an arranged marriage.

Immediately after Bassanio chooses the correct casket, Portia commits herself "to be directed | As from her lord, her governor, her king," and surrenders her property to him.

> Myself, and what is mine, to you and yours
> Is now converted. But now I was the lord
> Of this fair mansion, master of my servants,
> Queen o'er myself: and even now but now,
> This house, these servants, and this same myself
> Are yours, my lord's.

> (3.2.166–71)

Far from regretting this giving up of everything, Portia, in loving Bassanio, has already anticipated it. Just before Bassanio attempts the casket test, Portia admits that she has already yielded herself up emotionally: "Mine own, I would say, but if mine, then yours | And so all yours!" (3.2.17–18). Only the casket test has stood between them, "put bars between the owners and their rights" (19), and now that Bassanio has successfully completed it, the bar is removed and she and her property are totally at her bridegroom's disposal.

Portia is not merely giving voice to a lover's enthusiasm here. She describes herself as subject to the English common law principle of coverture: a married woman was legally subsumed into her husband's "person," and her property rested in his hands during marriage. As Karen Newman remarks, Portia here restates what seems the routine patriarchal conception of marriage.[7] However, there were normally some restrictions on the husband's ability to exploit the property the wife brought into a marriage. He was not, for instance, allowed to dispose of her freehold lands without her consent, although he could enjoy income from them during her lifetime. By the late sixteenth century, the courts of equity were in some circumstances further constraining a husband's control over his wife's property. Moreover, prosperous families, and many less prosperous ones, had devised ways to circumvent some of the possibly injurious rules of coverture, to prevent precisely the eventuality which Bassanio's past might threaten: the potential wasting of the bride's estate by a spendthrift husband. Amy Erickson has shown that the harsh provisions of coverture in fact had the effect of sharpening the attention of women and their families to the property consequences of marriage. As a result, even women in quite humble circumstances, or their fathers, frequently vested their property rights in a male trustee before the marriage was contracted, thus securing that property to the wife's use or at least restricting her husband's access to it.[8] In Ben Jonson's *Bartholomew Fair*, the law-student Quarlous cautions Winwife about this common tactic: having married an elderly widow for her money, Quarlous advises, Winwife may find that she "ha' conveyed her state safe enough from thee" (1.3.100–1). These legal niceties might seem too complex for a romantic comedy, were it not that a similar arrangement is in fact devised late in *The Merchant of Venice,* when Shylock is forced to consent to the setting up of such a trust for Jessica and Lorenzo, to be administered by Antonio.

In other words, while a real-life Bassanio could certainly improve his situation in life by marrying a wealthy woman, and he could exercise more power over his wife and her goods than would be the case in the twenty-first century, the wholesale, unconditional transfer of her property into his power would likely not have occurred. Portia's subjection to coverture, then, resembles Antonio's failure to buy marine insurance, in that it raises dramatic suspense by making tremendous consequences hang on apparently fortuitous events—chances, accidents, lucky responses to riddles.

Arguably, however, what the real-life father of an heiress might attempt to control through a trust arrangement, Portia's father eccentrically controls through the medium of the casket test. If we compare the property transfer here to those we have already seen in the history plays, we see more clearly the precise problem that the casket test is designed to solve. A father's property passes "naturally" to his eldest son in what I have called a principle of minimal alteration: the son "stands in the shoes of his ancestor" as a near replica of the former possessor. But in a system of coverture marriage, the wealth of a man with a daughter passes *through* the daughter and into the hands of the son-in-law. And the son-in-law does not—should not—duplicate the father insofar, if the union is not to be incestuous, as the son-in-law cannot be the father's child. Thus Edmund Plowden explains the preference for a male heir, and the plight of a man without one:

> if his inheritance should come to a female, in all probability she would take a husband…and consequently she and the whole inheritance would be subject to the will of a stranger, and be governed by him…and no man would willingly suffer

a stranger to reap the fruits of his labor, and therefore...the want of an heir male is a great grief.[9]

It's not clear exactly when Shakespeare wrote *The Merchant of Venice*, but most scholars place its composition between late 1596 and mid-1597, which would mean that the author was himself mourning this "want." Shakespeare's only son Hamnet had perished, probably of the plague, in August 1596, leaving Shakespeare the father of two surviving daughters. Shakespeare's wife, who was around forty years old, was likely at or close to the end of her fertile years; at any rate, the couple produced no more children, and Shakespeare may have been aware that he would eventually confront a practical dilemma similar to that shared by Shylock and by Portia's father.

In *The Merchant of Venice*, the casket test attempts not to regulate or restrict the flow of wealth from father to son-in-law, as a trust would do, but instead to restrict who is permitted to be the son-in-law. Bassanio can become Portia's father's heir because, contemplating the three caskets, he proves himself able to reconstruct Portia's father's train of reasoning. Portia's father's mind and Bassanio's mind work in the same way. Portia's father thus confidently leaves both wealth and daughter vulnerable to coverture because, by demonstrating this resemblance, Bassanio shows that unlike Morocco or Aragon he is not really a "stranger." At the end of *The Merchant of Venice*, Bassanio stands in the shoes of his wife's ancestor.

In other words, the principle of minimal alteration that enjoins primogeniture in families with sons still applies in this case. Bassanio establishes himself as a replica not in blood but in spirit. Moreover the specific way in which Bassanio resembles Portia's father is in his intuitive understanding of a paradoxical relationship between love and wealth. The trick to the casket test is that the man who does not value what is apparently valuable, who does not try to calculate his deserts, who declares himself willing to give without knowing whether he will receive in return, is the one who passes the test and wins the prize. The successful candidate gets the gold and silver by knowing not to seem to want it too much. By being able to overlook or at least temporarily bracket questions of material advantage, he derives material advantage. It is possible to construe this irony as merely bad faith or hypocrisy—plenty of critics have condemned Bassanio as an opportunistic fortune-hunter. Yet if there is, as Shell says, "commensurability (even identity) of men and money"[10] here, it is a commensurability that disallows itself even as it makes the equation. The casket test is the device of a man for whom spiritual resemblance emphatically trumps blood kinship, net worth, or other obvious material qualifications.

Jessica's marriage to Lorenzo involves some of the same issues as Portia's to Bassanio, since by the end of the play Shylock's wealth has passed through his daughter to his new son-in-law. But while Portia's father, lacking an "heir male of the body," devises an unconventional means to select a "son" who replicates him spiritually, Jessica's father has apparently made no plans at all to part with her. Shylock's material retentiveness—"fast bind, fast find"—extends to his daughter, whom he seems to expect to perform, indefinitely, the domestic functions that were at one time the purview of his late wife. It's therefore possible to see Shylock's reaction to Jessica's elopement both as an understandable reaction to the loss of his "own"—his daughter and his ducats, both considered as his property—but also as the unreasonable perpetuation of parental authority past its expiration date. As Solanio comments, "Shylock for his own part knew the bird was fledge, and that it is the complexion of them all to leave the dam" (3.1.25–7). Still, a daughter's maturity poses greater difficulty for a father—especially a miserly father like Shylock—than does a son's. A son inherits from the father only after the father's death, when the father has no more use for his own possessions. As we have seen in the *Henry IV* plays, the need to wait for the paternal demise can create an awkward situation for the adult son, the "heir apparent" whose resources are all still pending, but in the meantime it leaves the living father's resources undisturbed. The daughter, by contrast, receives her inheritance upon marriage, often when her father is still alive, so that her entitlement seems to deprive the father, and the birth family, of resources that they would otherwise still be able to use. The sense of the father's deprivation is all the more lively in a radically exogamous union like Jessica's, which apparently precludes further relations with her birth family or the sharing of wealth between them.

Both Portia's marriage and Jessica's, then, raise in different ways the question of a daughter's entitlement to a parent's property. As we have seen in the case of Prince Hal, for an eldest son succeeding to entailed lands the principle of primogeniture sheltered his inheritance from his father's misgivings. But the situation was different for younger sons, for daughters, or for heirs of families who held their wealth primarily in chattels (as did all Jews, since in most parts of Europe they were prohibited from acquiring land). Chattel wealth, as we have seen, could normally be sold or bequeathed however its owner pleased; "heirs of the body" received no automatic legal access to a parent's wealth. Because Shylock's wealth is entirely in chattels, Jessica can abscond with it, as she could not with a landed estate. Yet because his wealth is in chattels, thus not entailed upon the issue of his body, that property is in law entirely his to dispose of. In consequence Jessica's appropriation may seem especially presumptuous, a deliberate defiance of what she perfectly well knows is her father's will.

On the other hand, Jessica's sense of entitlement is not entirely unreasonable. The provision of a "portion" to daughters and younger sons, though not legally guaranteed, was customarily considered both as the children's due and as in the birth family's best interest, as it enabled those children to make strategic alliances with suitably prestigious families. Even families with an eldest son upon whom to focus their dynastic ambitions were reluctant to scant the daughters and younger sons entirely. Writes John Habakkuk, of the great landed families of a slightly later period:

> The portions of daughters were particularly important, not only because they were the subject of gossip and were a measure of the social standing of the family, but because they helped determine the kinship alliances which were the basis of social and political life of landed society. Fathers therefore had an incentive not merely to conform on this point to the norms of the social group but to provide sufficient endowment to enable their daughters to make acceptable unions.[11]

Custom could enforce what law could not, though since the force of custom only exerts itself upon those who care about "the norms of the social group," it has only tenuous power over outsiders like Shylock. Moreover, what counts as suitable provision for women in a patrilineal society is open to question. Eileen Spring shows that there were far fewer heiresses, especially in landed families, than demographic calculations would lead one to expect if the provisions of common law had been routinely observed. In fact, families figured out ways to circumvent common-law rules and settle the main inheritance upon a collateral male—an uncle or a nephew—rather than let it descend to a daughter who should have been the direct heir, providing her instead with a cash "portion" that was much less valuable than the estate to which she was theoretically entitled.[12] In Portia's and in Jessica's cases, however, no collateral male relatives seem to exist; Portia is already mistress of Belmont, and Jessica is the presumptive heir of Shylock. There is no alternative.

So what is the upshot of all these considerations? Jessica's escape with some of her father's property might be seen not as a commonplace larceny but as the theft of a marriage portion that, in normal circumstances, would have been her due. True, her receipt of that portion would be ordinarily be contingent upon her father's goodwill, which she knows that she forfeits by wedding a Christian. On the other hand, English law prevented non-believers from using their wealth to keep their heirs from converting to the majority faith. In Elizabethan England, making the open practice of Catholicism tantamount to treason meant that, at least in theory, Catholic property all reverted to the Crown and could be redistributed at the Queen's pleasure: surely a disincentive for any Catholic father wishing to disinherit a child on the grounds of conversion to the Church of England. Even a hundred years after Shakespeare's death, when English society had become somewhat more tolerant of religious difference, the property rights of religious minorities remained the subject of discriminatory legislation. After the number of Jews in England began to increase in the latter part of the seventeenth century, an Act was passed "to oblige Jews to maintain and provide for their Protestant children," preventing them from disinheriting their children if they, like Jessica, converted or married non-Jews.[13] So it is questionable whether Shakespeare or his original audience would have seen Jessica's depredations as indefensible. At the end of the trial scene, Shylock is forced to agree to an arrangement very like one he might have proposed himself had he approved of Jessica's choice of husband: a grant of half his property toward the establishment of the new family, and the promise of the remainder upon his death. His deed of gift, in other words, retrospectively regularizes Jessica's marriage by endorsing the legitimacy of her, and her husband's, claim upon his property.

Both Jessica's and Portia's marriages, then, are sustained by wealth that descends from the wife's kindred, wealth that departs from her birth family to become subsumed by her husband. In *The Merchant of Venice*, a biblical prototype of this arrangement is adumbrated in the story of Jacob and Laban recalled at length by Shylock in Act 2 scene 1. This retelling is part of a tissue of references to events in the life of Jacob (Genesis 19–36), including the impersonation of his brother Esau and the theft of Esau's blessing from their father Isaac, parodied in Launcelot Gobbo's tricking of his own father.[14] Jacob's sojourn with Laban is, in fact, the consequence of his strife with Esau: his mother sends him away to escape Esau's murderous rage. Laban is Jacob's maternal uncle, and he welcomes his nephew with a joyful recognition of their kinship: "surely you are my bone and my flesh!" Yet after agreeing to reward seven years of Jacob's labor with the gift of his beautiful daughter Rachel, he substitutes the ugly daughter Leah for Rachel in the dark, in what seems like a karmic retribution for Jacob's theft of Esau's blessing from the blind Isaac. Jacob must serve Laban for seven years longer in order to secure a marriage with Rachel. Thereafter Laban and Jacob make a deal: Jacob will herd Laban's sheep in return for the spotted lambs born of the flock. But Laban attempts to minimize the likelihood of his son-in-law's profiting by placing all his spotted sheep a considerable distance away, in the care of his own sons. Left with only solid-colored sheep, Jacob nevertheless gets the best of the bargain by controlling the circumstances under which the flocks are permitted to breed, yielding a surprising bounty of spotted lambs.

In *The Merchant of Venice*, Shylock and Antonio disagree about whether this outcome is ascribable to Jacob's cunning or to "the hand of heaven" (1.3.89). But in either case, Jacob's wealth undeniably derives from Laban's. The relationship between father-in-law and son-in-law is shot through with ambivalent generosity and competitiveness, so that the principals alternately cooperate and struggle to defeat one another. The father-in-law needs the son-in-law to perpetuate his bloodline through his daughters, and the son-in-law needs the father-in-law's wealth to support those daughters and the children born from them. Yet despite an alliance of at least fifteen years, the father-in-law's loss seems the son-in-law's gain, and vice versa. The son-in-law seems to deflect the flow of wealth, to enact a swerve in the bloodline, repeated in the astonishing outcome of Jacob's sheep breeding, in which spotted lambs are strangely born from solid-colored parents.

The aftermath of the story of Laban's sheep hammers home the implications. As Jacob prospers, Laban's sons begin to grumble: "Jacob has taken what is our father's, and from what was our father's he has gained all this wealth." Laban's daughters, Rachel and Leah, see the situation differently: "Is there any portion or inheritance left to us in our father's house? Are we not regarded by him as foreigners? For he has sold us, and he has been using up the money given for us. All the property which God has taken away from our father belongs to us and to our children." Both Laban's sons and Laban's daughters, in other words, continue to see the relationship between father-in-law and son-in-law as an adversarial one, in which either Jacob figures as the thief of the family property, or Laban figures as a profiteer selling his daughters into slavery. At his wives' urging, Jacob eventually departs with his family and the flocks he has gained. Soon Laban overtakes them and trades recriminations with Jacob. The dispute is finally settled by the erecting of a cairn of stones that represents a boundary between persons, between families, and between property entitlements: "I will not pass over this heap to you," Laban declares, "and you will not pass over this heap and this pillar to me." The stone marker seems to indicate an absolute rupture, and indeed, Laban henceforth falls out of the story. He departs to his side of the barrier after he has "kissed his grandchildren and his daughters and blessed them." Yet the neat division of the stone marker belies a messy and incomplete parting. Unbenownst to Jacob, Rachel has secreted Laban's household gods in her camelbag, and successfully absconds with them into her new homeland. Jacob's wife undermines her father, the old patriarch, by allying herself with, helping create, a young one. Her intervention recalls the similarly subversive agency of Jacob's "wise mother" Sarah, who, operating without the patriarch's knowledge or consent, diverted the paternal blessing intended for the elder son Esau, to her younger, favorite son. The ambivalent relation among siblings, already tense with rivalry, is exacerbated by the women's penchant for evading the rules of patriarchy, flouting their apparent disempowerment and diverting wealth and blessings into a new channel.

The story of Jacob and Laban, then, raises the question of a daughter's entitlement to the goods of her birth family, an entitlement that can easily look like a theft, given that in marriage she passes to an alien kindred. It also raises questions about female agency in a society that theoretically seems organized around male power and male control of possessions, but in which actually the flow of wealth is determined again and again by the schemes of mothers and wives.

In *The Merchant of Venice*, these questions are particularly pointed in Jessica's case because her marriage to Lorenzo apparently precludes a relationship with her Jewish father: there seems to be no possibility of alliance and cooperation here. Yet as a result of the way gender, inheritance practices, and marital arrangements intertwine, *any* assertion of independent agency by the daughter can seem a betrayal of the father, This is not merely a relic of some outdated biblical practice, as we see if we compare critics' discussion of Jessica in *The Merchant of Venice* and of Prince Hal in the *Henry IV* plays. Even those who dislike Hal object more strongly to his rejection of Falstaff than to his disobedience of his father: the latter is generally explained away as youthful high spirits, blamed on King Henry's imperceptive heavy-handedness, or praised as entrepreneurial political strategizing. By contrast Jessica, whose prospects for happiness seems so much more limited than Prince Hal's and whose father is dramatically more controlling, is often ferociously excoriated for her faithlessness. (Arthur Quiller-Couch, for instance, calls her "bad and disloyal, unfilial, a thief; frivolous, greedy, without any more conscience than a cat and without even a cat's redeeming love of home."[15]) Even Portia, who scrupulously observes the terms of her father's casket test even though no earthly power could enforce her adherence to them, sometimes attracts criticism for, it may be, daring to drop clues into the song that accompanies Bassanio's casket test.[16] The double standard is blatant: a young man's liberty is to be indulged, even applauded, while the young woman's deserves reproof. Yet the critical truisms more likely reflect not so much a personal sexism, holding particular characters to inconsistent standards, but rather the structural sexism inhering in a patrilineal inheritance system that never quite comes to terms with the abrupt alienation of family wealth accompanying the marriage of a daughter.

Perhaps all marriages, scandalously, involve not the loving alliance of two kin groups but the theft of the bride's family gods. Janet Adelman points out, in the course of a brilliant analysis, that Jews and Christians interpret the biblical stories referenced in *The Merchant of Venice* in nearly opposite ways. For the Jews, the patriarchs are their literal ancestors, and the Book of Genesis recounts the process in which, over several generations, they were distinguished from and preferred over the Gentile nations. But Christian typologists routinely reinterpret the same stories, seeing themselves as the "spiritual" heirs of the patriarchs and thrusting the Jews into the position of the legally privileged, but nonetheless rejected, elder brother, Ishmael or Esau. The Christians read the stories as conveying the blessings of God upon themselves, the spiritual "younger brothers," rather than upon the Jews who were the literal descendants.[17] In other words, not only do the stories in Genesis raise questions about a father's disposition of his property and undermine the expected primacy of the eldest child, but the literal reading of the story and the "spiritual" reading of the story contradict one another, so that the Jew and the Christian change places. In this crossing and substitution, we see the same simultaneous assertion and disavowal of equivalency that we have been seeing in other contexts. On the one hand "spiritual" and "material" goods share the same structure and features, so that the blessing of the father conveys his wealth, both spiritual and material, upon the favored child. On the other hand spiritual goods seem different, even in some ways opposed, to "merely material" goods. In his conversation with Antonio, Shylock identifies with Jacob, the lineal father of the Jews, praising his "thrift" and comparing his selective sheep-breeding to his own usurious lending practices. But by the end of the play, betrayed by Jessica and out-tricked by Portia, he finds himself in the position of the father-in-law Laban, at whose expense Jacob has profited. His wealth is turned to the benefit of Lorenzo, now in Jacob's position. And to Lorenzo, Shylock's forced bounty seems like the manna that, for Jews, is the sign of God's favor to the Jews, and for Christians, the sign of God's favor to the Gentiles.

The Jews, as a people and a religion, were typically conceived both as the progenitors of Christianity and as an alien kin group, a hostile other. Shylock, like Laban, is both kin and enemy to his son-in-law, and the more enemy because the more closely akin. The Christians would like to think of themselves as having superseded

Judaism, but the supersession is incomplete. In other words, Christians are not, neatly, the "heirs" of the Jews, standing in the shoes of their ancestors after the Jews' demise. The promise passes to them not lineally, from a father to a son, but obliquely, as wealth passes through the daughter from a possibly still-living father-in-law to a son-in-law. The final resolution, in which Shylock is forcibly converted to Christianity, hales him willy-nilly into community with the Venetians. But the problem of the coexistence of Jews and Christians is not resolved. In Laurence Olivier's famous and much-imitated production of *The Merchant of Venice*, the offstage singing of kaddish at the end of the play implies that Shylock has died, and perhaps also that Jessica's incorporation into the world of the Christians remains imperfect. In a sense, though, this imagined ending lets everybody off the hook. The problem of the daughter generally, in a patrilineal system, is that property must be ceded to her upon her marriage, rather than upon her father's death. This transfer deprives the father and vests wealth in the son-in-law, but the father often remains on the sidelines, resentful of what he has had to yield up. The problem of Shylock is not that he is dead, but that he obstinately survives.

Notes

1 In *Shakespeare's Tudor History: A Study of Henry IV, parts 1 and 2* (Aldershot: Ashgate, 2001), T. A. McAlindon traces this reading of the second tetralogy to Hermann Ulrici's *Shakespeare's Dramatic Art*, originally published in German in 1839.

2 Shakespeare wrote *The Merchant of Venice* between July 1596 and July 1598, but exactly when in that period is not clear. For a short summary of the evidence for earlier in this range, see Jay Halio's introduction to *The Merchant of Venice* (Oxford: Clarendon, 1993), pp. 27–8. M. M. Mahood argues for a slightly later date (1597–8) in the introduction to the New Cambridge Edition of *Merchant* (Cambridge: Cambridge University Press, 2003), pp. 1–2. If Mahood is correct, then possibly *Merchant* was written just after, rather than just before, *1 Henry IV*.

3 Mark Shell, "The Wether and the Ewe: Verbal Usury in *The Merchant of Venice*," *Kenyon Review* 1:4 (1979): 65–72; Lars Engle, *Shakespearean Pragmatism: Market of his Time* (Chicago, IL: University of Chicago Press, 1993), pp. 77–106; David Landreth, *The Face of Mammon: The Matter of Money in English Renaissance Literature* (Oxford: Oxford University Press, 2012).

4 Harley Granville-Barker, "*The Merchant of Venice*," Prefaces to Shakespeare, Second Series (London: Sidgwick and Jackson, 1935), p. 67.

5 Shell, "The Wether and the Ewe"; Luke Wilson, "Drama and Marine Insurance in Shakespeare's London," in Constance Jordan and Karen Cunningham, eds., *The Law in Shakespeare* (London: Palgrave Macmillan, 2007), pp. 127–42.

6 Alan Stewart, "Shakespeare is Shylock: Letters of Credit in *The Merchant of Venice*," in *Shakespeare's Letters* (Oxford: Oxford University Press, 2008), pp. 155–92.

7 Karen Newman, "Portia's Ring: Unruly Women and the Structure of Exchange in *The Merchant of Venice*," *Shakespeare Quarterly* 38 (1987): 19–33.

8 Amy Louise Erickson, *Women and Property in Early Modern England* (London: Routledge, 1993). See also Tim Stretton, *Women Waging Law in Elizabethan England* (Cambridge: Cambridge University Press, 1998), especially pp. 1–42 and 101–54.

9 Edmund Plowden, Sharington vs. Strotton (1566), in *The Commentaries or Reports Containing Divers Cases upon Matters of Law* (London: S. Brooke, 1816), pp. 298–309 (p. 305).

10 Shell, "The Wether and the Ewe", p. 48.

11 John Habakkuk, *Marriage, Debt, and the Estates System: English Landownership 1650–1950* (Oxford: Clarendon Press, 1994), p. 63.

12 Eileen Spring, *Law, Land, and Family: Aristocratic Inheritance in England, 1300–1800* (Chapel Hill, NC: University of North Carolina Press, 1993).

13 1 Anne c 30, "An Act to oblige Jews to maintain and provide for their Protestant children," reproduced in H. S. Q. Henriques, *The Jews and English Law* (London: J. Jacobs, 1908), pp. 167–9. Along similar lines, in Ireland, if any child of a Catholic family converted to Protestantism, he immediately came into possession of all his father's property, and his father was demoted to a life tenant.

14 For a discussion of these references and their significance see Lawrence Danson, *The Harmonies of The Merchant of Venice* (New Haven, CT: Yale University Press, 1978), pp. 73–8 and Janet Adelman, *Blood Relations: Christian and Jew in the Merchant of Venice* (Chicago, IL: University of Chicago Press, 2008), pp. 51–7.

15 From the introduction to *The Merchant of Venice*, New Cambridge Edition, quoted by Danson in *The Harmonies of The Merchant of Venice*, p. 132.

16 This much-repeated claim seems to originate in J. Weiss's *Wit, Humour, and Shakespeare* (Boston, 1876), p. 312.

17 Janet Adelman, sorting out the complex relationship between Judaism and Christianity in the play, has pointed to the prominence of several other biblical stories of vexed inheritance in *The Merchant of Venice*, in addition to the story of Laban's sheep: the displacement of the bond-woman Hagar's child Ishmael by the freewoman Sarah's son Isaac, and, in the next generation, the displacement of the elder twin Esau by the younger twin Jacob.

4

The Properties of Friendship in *The Merchant of Venice*

At several critical junctures in *The Merchant of Venice*, characters propose divesting themselves of all that they possess. Asked by Bassanio for a loan, Antonio places at his disposal "My purse, my person, my extremest means" (1.1.138). At Belmont, Bassanio selects the casket that, as Morocco and Aragon have previously informed us, warns that "Who chooses me must give and hazard all he hath" (2.7.9; 2.9.20). Upon Bassanio's successful choice, as we have seen, Portia surrenders herself and her estate to him: "Myself and what is mine to you and yours | Is now converted" (3.2. 169–70). She wishes, in fact, that she only had more with which to endow her new husband:

> for you
> I would be trebled twenty times myself
> A thousand times more fair, ten thousand times more rich.
>
> (3.2.156–8)

Later in the play, in the face of Shylock's intransigence, Bassanio wishes he could give up everything on Antonio's behalf:

> Life itself, my wife, and all the world
> Are not with me esteemed above thy life.
> I would lose all—aye, sacrifice them all
> Here to this devil—to deliver you.
>
> (4.1.277–82)

Granted, none of these offers, scrutinized closely, are quite as impressively thoroughgoing as they seem. When Bassanio asks Antonio to bankroll his expedition to Belmont, Antonio's purse happens to be empty—"all my fortunes are at sea" (1.1.177). He eventually offers a pound of flesh as collateral for Shylock's loan, staking his person in place of, not in addition to, his purse. Along the same lines, a picayune audience member might wonder what, exactly, Bassanio "hath" either to give or to hazard, seeing that his journey to Belmont relies on funds borrowed from Shylock and guaranteed by Antonio's bond. For her part, Portia hedges the gift of herself and her estate by endowing Bassanio with a ring that he must safe-guard: both an additional gift and a condition placed upon the rest of her gifts. Finally, of course, when Bassanio offers his life, his wife, and all the world to save Antonio's life he must do so in the conditional, because, as he well knows, those sacrifices are neither what Shylock is seeking nor what the court will demand.

Despite these qualifications, all these characters seem compelled to offer everything to, or on behalf of, someone they love. "Every-thing" explicitly includes what we might call intrinsic qualities, "the self itself," as well as alienable property: Antonio's "purse and person," Portia's "myself and what is mine." What is at stake in these offers? Despite their superficial similarity, the property impli-cations are actually quite different in the different cases. In mar-riage, property relations are explicitly specified in law, and justified in terms of the purpose of the union: the rendering of male and female into "one flesh" in order to perpetuate the family and the species. Friendship, by contrast, is a looser, non-teleological, largely extra-legal concept. In early modern English, friends and kin are overlapping categories: thus in *Measure for Measure*, when Claudio refers to Juliet's "dower | Remaining in the coffer of her friends" (1.2.127–8), the friends in question are her parents, or those rela-tives who have control over her estate. "Friends" can also mean benefactors—patrons, supporters, anyone from whose acquaintance one can derive an advantage. Thus the "friends" Ben Jonson thanks in his preface to *Volpone* are the "commenders and favorers" who have furthered Jonson's career as a dramatist by applauding his play and praising his literary talent. Yet classical theorists of friend-ship such as Aristotle and Cicero, as well as their early modern humanist heirs, strenuously distinguish between a kind of friendship based upon family connections or upon material neediness, and one based upon the spiritual affinity of virtuous men for one another.[1]

"We agreed evermore in love, mind, purpose, and opinion, in which thing the whole pith of friendship standeth," says Laelius of his friendship with Scipio in Cicero's *De Amicitia*. This form of friendship does not necessarily eschew transfers of material goods, such as the money Antonio has lent to Bassanio, but those transfers are supposed to be of ancillary importance, and are entirely voluntary rather than legally enjoined.

Part of the appeal of such friendship, in fact, lies in its optional quality—its thrilling exercise of individual agency. Whereas, as Montaigne acidly notes, marriage "is a covenant which hath nothing free but the entrance, the continuance being forced and constrained,"[2] the sustaining of virtuous friendship, precisely because it receives no formal, institutional support, requires the continuous renewal of a choice. And the appearance of spirituality and freedom in ideal friendship is, in fact, a consequence of its relative subordination of property concerns. Montaigne remarks how competition over a patrimony often spoils even the most egalitarian blood kinship, the relation between siblings: "that the riches of one shall be the poverty of another, doth exceedingly distemper and distract all brotherly alliance, and conjunction." By contrast, because friendship does not necessarily imply property connections at all, it can flower without regard to the divisions of status, wealth, and blood that normally constrain other, less precious relationships: as Alan Bray remarks, "the potential strength of the [friends' role] lay in their very freedom from that expectation of inheritance."[3]

Yet the same features that make friendship so highly idealized in the period can also be profoundly unnerving. In the absence of clear guidelines, how are friends to know what they owe to one another? On the one hand, true friendship apparently disdains material calculation and eschews self-serving or self-regard, and even in its less ideal forms friends do not have clear-cut property obligations to one another. So, in a sense, friends owe one another nothing. On the other hand, it could also be said that they owe one another everything. "All things are common among friends" was already an old saw when Aristotle discussed it in the *Nichomachean Ethics*, and as the rhetoric of friendship becomes more heated in the early modern period, the question of what this common participation entails becomes a more pointed one. Montaigne construes the "commonness"

of friendly property in an especially comprehensive way, as including "All things …: wills, thoughts, judgments, goods, wives, children,
honor, and life." He associates the dissolving of property boundaries
in friendship with an ecstatic self-loss, a mutual "plunging" of each
soul into the other. Humanist writers frequently associate the generosity of friendship with the radical charity that Christianity enjoins
toward others. Christ's Passion, of course, is a paradigmatic example
of this absolute self-sacrifice, and as Alan Bray has noted, Christ was
often portrayed as the perfect friend.[4] Christianity mandates charity
to others not because they are particularly loveable or closely akin
or intimately known, or likely to render one any advantage, but
merely because they are fellow human beings. "Give to every man
that asketh of thee: and of him that taketh away thy goods, ask them
not again," advises Jesus (Luke 6.30).

Certainly the friends in *The Merchant of Venice* assume that the
relationship entails generosity; when one's friend demands a favor,
or a loan, or a ring, giving it to him seems almost an automatic
reflex.

> GRAZIANO Signor Bassanio.
> BASSANIO Graziano.
> GRAZIANO I have a suit to you.
> BASSANIO You have obtained it.
>
>   (2.2.158–9)

Only after promising to satisfy Graziano does Bassanio learn what
he wants. Even the poorest members of the Venetian community
attempt to participate in the rituals of gift-giving; Old Gobbo, for
instance, materializes at Shylock's door with a gift of doves, transferred to Bassanio, Launcelot's new employer. The use of liberal
gifts to solidify social connections suggests a difference between the
conceptions of prodigality in *The Merchant of Venice* and in the slightly
later *Henry IV* plays. Falstaff's prodigality, and potentially Prince
Hal's, is a form of dishonor insofar it is associated with a selfish rapa-
city that runs roughshod over other people's property entitlements;
Henry IV Part 1 features a highway robbery, *Part 2* Falstaff's fleecing
of Mistress Quickly and Justice Shallow. Bassanio, by contrast, uses
his borrowed wealth generously, if perhaps unwisely, for instance

providing Launcelot with an especially gaudy servant's livery out of a desire to indulge Launcelot rather than to please himself.

Unfortunately, for those who are not gods, unconditional generosity to everybody seems incompatible with an ordinary prudential concern for one's own continued thriving. In *The Merchant of Venice*, Christianity's demands for universal charity collide with limited human means and inclination. Moreover, it is not clear that reckless munificence is always a religious obligation. The parable of the prodigal son and its many Renaissance adaptations, after all, associate the son's squandering of his birthright with a gravely imprudent liberality to friends, as the son departs from his family in order to carouse with "companions" in a foreign land. Thus friendship, which Aristotle, Cicero, and those who follow them construe as absolutely basic to social and political life, and which Christianity makes fundamental to the community of believers, also has the potential dangerously or indiscriminately to dissolve the property boundaries between individuals, families, and groups.

Conscious of this threat, many writers are not so thoroughgoing as Montaigne, and attempt to reserve domains which are never to be breached in even the most unbridled friendly intimacy. In *De Amicitia*, for instance, Laelius argues that a virtuous man will not stoop to a discreditable action to benefit a friend; in *The Merchant of Venice*, Antonio similarly specifies that Bassanio's endeavors must "stand... | Within the eye of honor" (1.1.136–7) to receive his support, suggesting that there is a limit beyond which even his loyalty would not go. Romance plots, such as those Shakespeare adapts in *The Two Gentlemen of Verona*, *A Winter's Tale*, and *The Two Noble Kinsmen*, frequently specify a different limit, marking out the wife or mistress as the single thing apparently not shareable between friends.

So if generosity is a good thing, but unthinking, indiscriminate generosity is a dangerous thing, then criteria need to be specified that clarify who counts as a friend and what friends ought to receive. Yet exactly what those criteria might be, and conversely, what limit placed upon generosity suffices to destroy a friendship, remain uncertain. Here again the comparison with marriage is instructive. A false bridegroom or bride is disqualified by one of an explicit list of "impediments": a person who is already married, or is too closely akin by blood or marriage, or who is permanently impotent, or who is a member of a celibate religious order. Each of these impediments is a matter of fact, ascertainable in a court of law. By contrast, a false friend might be a conscious hypocrite, miming love in an attempt to gain some selfish advantage; or he might merely be someone whose conception of friendship's debts does not entirely correlate with his companion's, and thus who does not care to share that to which his friend believes himself entitled. The issue arises in many of Shakespeare's plays. What do the Prince and Falstaff owe one another in the *Henry IV* plays? What does Brutus owe Caesar in *Julius Caesar*? What does Timon owe his fellow Athenians in *Timon of Athens*, and what do they owe him in return? In all these plays, the friends find the obligations of the relationship in some way overtaxing, so that they limit them or attempt to shake them off, and when they do, their degree of culpability is debatable. The disputes among critics and audiences over Hal's treatment of Falstaff at the end of *Henry IV Part 2* are symptomatic of the problem: what to one critic seems like the Prince's hypocrisy or coldness, to another is evidence that he has his priorities straight. One imagines that for Prince Hal or Brutus or Timon it might be a relief if they could refer to the "bond" that Cordelia can reference with such tactless assurance at the beginning of *King Lear*: the Biblical mandates that on the one hand require the honoring of father and mother, and on the other hand clearly subordinate filial piety to marital love.

The uncertainty and legal unenforceability of the claims of friendship, and the way they shuttle between spiritual and material goods, create several interlinked problems. The first is the question of the number of one's friends. It is never quite clear how widely one ought to draw the circle of one's intimacy. Classically-inspired humanist texts tend to narrow the circuit severely, so that one has only one friend, a mirror-counterpart, and the intensity of the relationship prevents its being widely extended. "This perfect amity I speak of," writes Montaigne, "is indivisible; each man doth so wholly give himself unto his friend, that he hath nothing left him to divide elsewhere." If Montaigne places no apparent limit upon what kinds of goods might be shared among friends, he compensates by placing a very strict limit on how many persons to share them with.

As we have seen, however, in common early modern usage the word "friend" could simply signify "associate." Set against the exclusive, closed conception of ideal friendship celebrated by Renaissance moral philosophers are the more extensive and ramifying associations that actually characterize the world of *The Merchant of Venice*. Bassanio is Antonio's friend, but so are Graziano, Lorenzo, Salanio, and Salerio. As we have seen, even married couples in the play do not form self-sufficient dyads, since their wealth is contributed, willingly or not, by the brides' fathers. Likewise, but in a more thoroughgoing and intentional way, the friendship between Antonio and Bassanio must venture outside itself, to Shylock and to Portia, to acquire the things it apparently needs to sustain it. This pattern, in which a dyadic relationship proves inadequate by itself, and therefore seeks supplementation, is repeated so many times in *The Merchant of Venice* that eventually it seems the basis of social life itself. Transactions that involve couples of various descriptions—two friends, a husband and wife, a father and daughter, a ruler and subject—inevitably pull additional persons into their orbit. Bassanio asks Antonio for a sum of money, but Antonio does not have it on hand; he therefore obtains a loan from Shylock, who obtains part of the funds from Tubal. Bassanio courts Portia, but he needs to win not her consent, but Portia's dead father's, through the medium of the casket test—which, it turns out, also determines the marital fortunes of Bassanio's friend, Graziano, and Portia's companion, Nerissa. Shylock demands justice from the Duke; the Duke, instead of simply rendering it, consults Bellario, who sends his substitute Balthasar, who interprets the law so that Shylock's fate is ultimately in the hands not of the Duke but of Antonio. Balthasar requests Bassanio's ring, and Bassanio eventually relinquishes it at Antonio's insistence, not directly but by a messenger; when Portia discovers that the ring is missing, Antonio once more stands surety for Bassanio, this time pledging his soul rather than his body. In the world of *The Merchant of Venice*, nobody, and no simple coalition of two persons either, turns out to be "sufficient," either as a purse or as a person, but requires enhancement by what others can provide.

In other words, the need for supplementation disrupts the dyad even as it enriches it, forcing it to veer from simple mirroring or reciprocity into complicated transfers, duplications, supplantings, and goings-between, and creating multifarious credit relations in which persons put themselves formally or informally in one another's debt. The networks thus created in *The Merchant of Venice* recall the actual early modern commercial communities studied in painstaking detail by Craig Muldrew, in which every individual and each trading relationship was enmeshed in a larger web of emotional and economic transactions.[5] In the credit economy that results, in which wealth is not so much possessed as kept restlessly in circulation, one's ability to command resources becomes a function not merely of what one has on hand at any given moment, but of what one potentially owns. For assessing creditworthiness, not merely a person's wealth but the strength of his connection to a network of friends becomes a salient factor.

If the couple is too limited in its resources to survive alone, and a principled generosity to everyone is so demanding as to be unworkable, then perhaps friendship must locate itself as an intermediate term between the dyad and the entire community considered as an indiscriminate whole. How might it do so? In *The Merchant of Venice*, two property transfers help delineate this intermediate status. Shylock's loan of three thousand ducats to Antonio discriminates friendship from commercial or business transactions, and also from intense but non-loving relationships. Portia's ring trick discriminates friendship from marriage, which can be entered into with only one specified, other-sex individual at a time.

What exactly is at stake in the bond between Antonio and Shylock? Extending a loan to a person in need without expecting a usurious profit is, Antonio believes, his civic and religious duty: "for when did friendship take | A breed for barren metal of his friend?" (1.3.128–9). He articulates the common principle that friendship ought not be self-seeking or profit-oriented, but ought to attend only to the needs of the person seeking succor. Many people, apparently, count as friends to Antonio, since he extends interest-free loans so openhandedly that, according to Shylock, he "brings down the rate of usance here in Venice" (1.3.40). Yet when Antonio requires a loan himself, none of his Christian associates are apparently willing to return the favor. "Go forth— | Try what my credit can in Venice do," he tells Bassanio (1.1.179–80). But next we see them, they are already negotiating with the Jew, presumably having been rebuffed by those upon whom Antonio's only claim is a vaguely-defined, extralegal duty of friendly reciprocation.

The way to obtain a loan in *The Merchant of Venice* seems to be not to rely upon favors but to appeal instead to a commercial lender. While friends are supposed to renounce scorekeeping in the name of emotional and material generosity, business transactions involve explicit, quid pro quo exchanges of property, exchanges predicated not upon mutual generosity but upon calculation and self-interest. The usurer insists, in other words, upon making a profit by providing resources that friends should perhaps, but do not always, offer spontaneously and without an eye to their own advantage. The usurer stands in the place of the friend—or rather, in the place the friend ought to occupy but has left vacant—but he does not do so for "friendly" or generous reasons. His very existence, in fact, demonstrates the comparative frailness of concept of friendly obligation. For this reason the usurer is easy to hate: palpably a villain yet at the same time somehow deceptively attractive, in that despite the obviousness of his stigma he *resembles* a friend, and is therefore blamable as a hypocrite. Antonio calls Shylock "a goodly apple rotten at the heart" (1.3.93) and takes pains to differentiate his own lending practices from Shylock's calculating approach. For his part, Shylock claims in his transactions with Christians to focus frankly and exclusively upon the value of his client's alienable property, sidestepping questions of personal compatibility. When Antonio and Bassanio approach Shylock for a loan, Shylock observes, "Antonio is a good man." "Have you heard any imputation to the contrary?" replies Bassanio testily, assuming that Shylock is questioning Antonio's integrity. "Ho no no no no," clarifies Shylock, "my meaning in saying he is a good man is to have you understand me that he is sufficient" (1.3.11–14). In fact, Antonio interferes with Shylock's business dealings and subjects him to gross anti-Semitic abuse. Yet as a commercial prospect, Antonio is "good" so long as his wealth suffices, regardless of Shylock's assessment of his character.

This radical restriction and diminution of the ethical category, "good," is exactly what offends friendship theorists about any overlap between friendship and self-interest. Yet of course the commercial transaction, apparently devoid of sentiment, offers some major advantages. Shylock's willingness to loan money at interest efficiently serves both parties, supplying the immediate needs of the borrower while guaranteeing an eventual profit to the lender. Moreover, the suspension of the need for goodwill or personal approval permits commercial transactions among people with disparate values, belief systems, and customs—between Christians and Jews, for instance. Shylock describes how he restricts his dealings with Christians to business interactions: "I will buy with you, sell with you, walk with you, talk with you, and so following, but I will not eat with you, drink with you, nor pray with you" (1.3.29–31). Buying and selling simply need not entail fellowship, religious conformity, or mutual esteem.

Friendship theorists regard commercial relationships as morally suspect, in that they concern themselves with contingent rather than intrinsic qualities of a person. Antonio, to a usurer, is "good" insofar as he owns sufficient property; without property, he is no longer "good." By the same token, this standard of goodness can be met by anyone possessing equal resources. Characteristic of "love," by contrast—both friendly love and romantic love—is the impulse to single out loved persons not for what they own but for what they are, and to construe this singularity as fundamental to the relationship. The Book of Common Prayer requires each party to marriage vows to name the other reciprocally: "I take thee N to my wedded wife," "I take thee N to my wedded husband." This specific, non-interchangeable individual is "taken," moreover, "for better, for worse, for richer, for poorer, in sickness and in health," that is, regardless of circumstances and despite the ways in which those circumstances might change in the future. Even if, at some later date, the relationship no longer serves the self-interest of one or both of the parties, it must still be perpetuated "till death us depart." In my first chapter, I quoted the young lover Fenton, in *The Merry Wives of Windsor,* contrasting his initial attraction to Anne "as a property" with his eventual love for "the very riches of thyself." Wanting her as a property means loving her only *for* her property, that is, instrumentally, as a means to an end outside herself. "True" love, by contrast, still values "riches," but riches differently defined, as characteristics that are deep-rooted and apparently inalienable attributes of "thyself."

This kind of love, however, creates a crisis of valuation, because it seems to defy market imperatives. The prices of commodities are determined by what buyers are willing to pay—that is, by an entire community's consensus about their worth. In *The Merchant of Venice*, the golden casket is a paradigmatic instance of this kind of valuable object: it is "what many men desire." By contrast romantic love and "true" single-sex friendship each invest the beloved with a value often visible to the lover alone. As Francis Bacon observes, "the speaking in perpetual hyperbole is comely in nothing but in love...For there was never proud man thought so absurdly well of himself as the lover doth of the person loved."[6] A lover's hyperbole is the rhetorical consequence of the idiosyncratic overvaluation of one person in comparison to another. "What makes him or her so remarkable?" wonder the bystanders, while the lover seems to rave. Indeed, the intuition of the beloved's preciousness is almost the paradigmatic case of something that cannot be assimilated to market value, something excessive and inexplicable to others.

Just as love dispenses with prudential calculation and with shared, "reasonable" ideas about fungibility and comparable worth, so does hatred. And this brings us back to Shylock's bond with Antonio. Initially, as we have seen, Shylock features in *The Merchant of Venice* as "the usurer," and the successful solicitation of Shylock thus seems contrasted with the presumably earlier, unsuccessful solicitations of friends, as a commercial or business relationship rather than a form of intimacy. Venice is a busy trading entrepôt, and we hear that "the trade and profit of the city | Consisteth of all nations" (3.3.30–1). Antonio and Shylock, in their different ways, have made their fortunes in commerce and are thus presumably skilled dealmakers. Yet this impression of business acumen turns out to be erroneous, or at least irrelevant to the situation at hand. For the commercial trappings of the relationship between Shylock and Antonio are largely deceptive window-dressing on a transaction motivated, on Antonio's side, by an apparently irrational desire to advance Bassanio's fortunes, and on Shylock's side, from a rooted hatred of Antonio that Shylock articulates to the audience in advance of the conversation: "If I can catch him once upon the hip | I will feed fat the ancient grudge I bear him" (1.3.41–2). If there are no "pure" love relationships in *The Merchant of Venice*, untouched by material considerations, neither do we see any ordinary, sensible commercial transactions, for which material self-interest is the only or even the primary criterion.[7]

Shylock offers Antonio not a loan on normal usurious terms, but a loan secured by a pound of flesh. The Christians respond to his outlandish proposal with an uncertainty about whether to consider it an outrage ("You shall not seal to such a bond for me!" Bassanio tells Antonio) or a joke, a "merry sport." Shylock encourages the latter construal by emphasizing the proposal's commercial absurdity: "A pound of a man's flesh taken from a man | Is not so estimable, profitable neither | As flesh of muttons, beefs, or goats" (1.3.161–3). This lack of exchange value constitutes a form of reassurance, encouraging Antonio and Bassanio to take as "kindness" what is actually anything but.

What Shylock leaves unspoken, of course, is that not only kindness but enmity dispenses with considerations of self-interest and of communal determinations of relative value. Later, in court, Shylock is offered the bond, twice the bond, ten times the bond, but refuses no matter what the incentive to convert his injury into a prudent calculation of damages.

> You ask me why I rather choose to have
> A weight of carrion flesh, than to receive
> Three thousand ducats. I'll not answer that,
> But say it is my humor.
> . . .
> So I can give no reason, nor I will not,
> More than a lodged hate and certain loathing
> I bear Antonio.

$$(4.1.39\text{--}60)$$

The idiosyncratic and excessive valuations of both enmity and love flagrantly disregard normal parameters of profit and loss. Enmity and friendship share too a refusal to accept substitutes: to see persons or items as fungible. In consequence hatred has the same relationship to an apparently intrinsic selfhood that love does. That is why it is easy to mistake for, or misrepresent as, "kindness." "Hath not a Jew eyes?" asks Shylock, in a speech famous for its eloquent enumeration of shared human attributes. Yet the rhetorical flourish that would ordinarily precede an appeal to empathetic fellow-feeling here precedes a determination to revenge, suggesting the way violent antipathy, like love, involves a hyperbolic, irrationally charged relation between specific persons.

If the problem shared by both friendship and enmity is a problem of how to define what one person might properly owe to another, then conceivably a written contract might helpfully tame the immoderate whims of individuals by specifying the limits of those obligations. Yet Shylock's bond with Antonio exacerbates rather than defuses the exorbitancy of their relationship. The bond takes a pound of Antonio's flesh as collateral for three thousand ducats. If Antonio's flesh is less vendible than goat meat or beef, but on the other hand, Antonio requires it for life, then how should its value be assessed? In what sense is a pound of flesh "worth" three thousand ducats?

Henry S. Turner observes, "Shylock's demand...is precisely for a pound that both *is* and *is not* 'body,' a pound that can be measured out, removed, and separated from Antonio....but a pound that assumes its significance precisely by remaining 'part,' by remaining integrated *and* distinct at the same time."[8] The conundrum of value vividly literalizes the problem of property as both self and not-self, intrinsic and alienable, which I have already discussed in my first chapter and elsewhere. The "pound of flesh" transaction thus neatly specifies a triangular comparison among friendship, enmity, and commercial relations. In both commerce and enmity, "love" is absent, but for different reasons and to different ends. The commercial relation resembles friendship in its provision of benefits for both parties, but it is motivated by selfishness rather than by generosity, and it is easily transferable from one party to another, similarly situated one. Enmity, on the other hand, retains exactly the passionately wholehearted, non-fungible quality of friendship that the commercial transaction lacks, focusing on inalienable rather than alienable attributes, but reverses, of course, the emotional valence, substituting inordinate hatred for inordinate love.

By the end of the courtroom scene (Act 4 scene 1), Shylock has been defeated, the prospect of revenge that he represented has been eliminated, and the friendship between Antonio and Bassanio apparently "saved" from the threats posed to it both by enmity and by commerce, or by rather by enmity disguised as commerce. Yet the question of the relation between *marriage* and friendship still remains unaddressed. This relation becomes the theme of Portia's ring trick. Like Antonio's pound of flesh, Portia's ring seems an especially fraught item of property. The wedding or betrothal ring symbolizes a couple's unbreakable connection, in an era in which divorce is impossible. That symbolic significance, so in excess of and apparently different in kind from the ring's value as a marketable commodity, is what Nerissa refers to when she chides Graziano for pointing out that his ring was a cheap one: "What talk you of the posy or the value?" (5.1.150). It is what Jessica disregards when she exchanges Leah's turquoise for a monkey, ignorantly or callously violating her father's memory of his youthful courtship. Because Shylock's love for Leah is non-fungible, the ring cannot be assigned a monkey equivalent, even an infinite wilderness of monkeys.

Thus Portia's ring, like Antonio's pound of flesh, is a material object that ironically embodies the idea of a relationship supposedly transcending "mere" material considerations. But it does so from the opposite direction, so to speak. For whereas Shylock's bond declares an inalienable possession, flesh, to be alienable property, Portia's ring is a manifestly alienable chattel declared to be henceforth inalienable. Whereas the problem of Antonio's flesh is that it is too firmly attached, the problem of the ring is that it is dangerously unfixed. What keeps it on Bassanio's finger is not anatomical constraint but the exercise of Bassanio's will.

And of course, Bassanio loses the ring almost immediately. Portia bestows a ring upon him, contrives to extract it from him, and berates him for parting with it, before finally revealing herself to have been the young lawyer Balthasar, and the ring's actual recipient. What is the point of this rigmarole? Critics since W. H. Auden have often assumed that marriage and friendship in the play must be at odds, and that Bassanio's marriage to Portia is incompatible with his friendship with Antonio. Auden imagines the merchant of Venice as a tragic homosexual: "the married couples must enter the lighted house and leave Antonio standing alone on the darkened stage, outside the Eden from which, not by the choice of others, but by his own nature, he is excluded."[9] In this reading the ring trick is Portia's cleverly heartless way of dismissing Antonio from Bassanio's life.

Thus Alan Sinfield writes: "The last act of the play is Portia's assertion of her right to Bassanio. Her strategy is purposefully heterosexist: in disallowing Antonio's sacrifice as a plausible reason for parting with the ring, she disallows the entire seriousness of male love."[10] Certainly in other plays, Shakespeare shows same-sex bonds explicitly challenged by heterosexual coupling: *The Two Gentlemen of Verona, A Midsummer Night's Dream, Romeo and Juliet,* and *Much Ado About Nothing* are a few examples. Yet in *The Merchant of Venice* there is no textual evidence that Portia resents Antonio—Antonio's supposed defeat and frustration need therefore to be represented onstage by non-verbal means, such as Auden's imagined staging. Shakespeare's text registers, in fact, the opposite sentiments. Antonio bankrolls Bassanio's trip to Belmont—from which he himself will profit, as Bassanio points out, if Bassanio succeeds—and encourages his friend to do everything he possibly can to ingratiate himself with his intended bride. When Bassanio reveals Antonio's plight, Portia urges him to rush to the aid of "a friend of such description," delaying the consummation of her marriage and providing the funds that, she has every reason to believe, Shylock will accept to discharge the bond. She journeys to Venice, saves Antonio's life, and afterward welcomes Antonio to Belmont, delivering to him the news that his ships have literally come in. Not surprisingly, then, Antonio's last words in the play are effusive thanks to Portia: "sweet lady, you have given me life and living" (5.1.285). Finally, when Antonio promises Portia—"my soul upon the forfeit"—that Bassanio "will never more break faith advisedly" (5.1.251–2), that promise would seem to require him not to vanish from Bassanio's life but to remain there, monitoring his behavior.

It's possible, of course, to read all this as freighted with heavy irony: to understand Antonio's generosity as profoundly self-sabotaging, masochistic, or passive-aggressive, and to read Portia's generosity as simply aggressive, intended to place Antonio so uncomfortably in her debt that he will be happy to cede any claims he has upon Bassanio.[11] But what the text seems most straightforwardly to indicate is that Portia does not view Antonio as a threat or a rival. Possibly critics have been too quick to interpret the ring trick as a way of manipulating Bassanio's emotional allegiances because they assume that these allegiances must be undivided, so that if he has a wife he cannot have a friend, and vice versa. Yet everything we know about marriage and friendship in the early modern period indicates that, in fact, married persons did not feel themselves obliged to abandon their friends of the same sex.[12]

If the ring trick is not a way to send Antonio packing, what is it? Perhaps it is a lesson in property management. In early modern Europe, rings were exchanged not only between lovers and betrothed couples, but also as mementos among friends. Like wedding rings, friendship rings betoken affection, but the ethics of their retention are different, because instead of signifying monogamous attachment, they can circulate strategically as a way of solidifying warm feelings among persons whose close relationships are not imagined to be necessarily exclusive. Thus Antonio, like Portia, conceives of the ring as a symbolic gift, not a commodity, but one that can and indeed should be given away when occasion serves.[13] Just as he has generously facilitated Bassanio's courtship, Antonio expects Bassanio generously to requite the young lawyer who has saved his life, and who now declines a fee: who insists, in other words, upon putting their relationship on a friendly rather than a commercial basis. For the bride Portia, retaining the ring demonstrates that the wearer prizes the relationship it signifies over its commercial value. For the friend Antonio, by contrast, retaining the ring amounts to a niggardly assertion that, as a piece of "mere" chattel property, it is more valuable than the prospect of enlarging the circle of friendship to include a deserving new member.

When Portia-as-Balthasar demands Bassanio's ring, in other words, she entangles Bassanio in two opposite strategies for the management of symbolically fraught "relationship property:" an ethics of retention competes with an ethics of liberality. Not surprisingly, Bassanio is perplexed as to the right course of action, first insisting upon keeping the ring, but afterwards yielding it up. He describes his eventual capitulation to Balthasar's demand and Antonio's entreaty:

> I was enforced to send it after him.
> I was beset with shame and courtesy;
> My honor would not let ingratitude
> So much besmear it.

> (5.1.215–18)

Bassanio is overwhelmed with the painful conviction that his honor is on the line precisely because gratitude to friends is not legally coerced, and that therefore his behavior in this case displays his character. Bassanio's susceptibility to shame and his sensitivity to the claims of honor and courtesy are, in one respect, very good signs for Portia, since the main safeguard of a married woman under coverture was the man's sense of responsibility for her. Here, his honor demands that the friend be gratified.

Still, what looks like honorable liberality from one perspective looks offensive and wasteful from another. The casket test has selected a mate for Portia who embraces risk and who is careless of his own material advantage: both attractive traits, yet dangerous in some circumstances. Portia therefore wants—nay, urgently needs—to educate her heedless bridegroom in an unfamiliar way of thinking, and so she seizes her last chance, in the fortuitously extended time between wedding vows and consummation, when she still possesses legal agency independent of Bassanio.

What, exactly, must Bassanio learn? The indissolubility of the marriage vow, the absence of reliable means to restrain or assist fertility, the coverture of women, the exclusion of bastards from inheritance, all make early modern marriage a very different institution from its twenty-first century counterpart—and different, as well, from early modern friendship. As Laurie Shannon remarks, "Whether we consider the tensions between friendship and marriage so often laid out in period texts... or instead, assess the politics of a classically derived, same-sex friendship idea as an alternative polity of consensual equals, the tropes of affect proposed by marital and friendship discourses diverge—utterly."[14] This "utter" divergence is somewhat modified, as Shannon goes on to acknowledge, in the emergent ideology of companionate marriage which Shakespeare's comic endings seem designed to celebrate, for those endings suggest that successful matrimony involves an emotional intimacy that might grow out of the sexual connection between husband and wife. Although Portia does not need to displace Antonio from Bassanio's affections, she may well want to access for her marriage some of the emotional advantages traditionally offered by friendship between men. Nonetheless, it is not "heterosexist" to acknowledge, as Renaissance writers on the topic almost universally do, that property figures very differently in marriage than in friendship. Early modern marriage joins property to blood by safeguarding them both: the man controls the marital property, "husbanding" it wisely, while the wife, meanwhile, protects the bloodline by remaining sexually faithful. Marriage requires these safekeepings not because it is necessarily better or higher or more intimate than "male love" but because safekeeping is intrinsic to its reproductive teleology, from which single-sex friendship is perhaps blessedly free. This understanding of the marriage bond explains the precise tenor of Portia's reproaches: when Bassanio violates his vow to keep safe the property entrusted to him, Portia threatens to violate hers to safeguard the blood, declaring that she will revenge herself on Bassanio by sleeping with the doctor.

> I will become as liberal as you,
> I'll not deny him anything I have,
> No, not my body nor my husband's bed.
>
> (5.1.225–7)

In Portia's formulation, adultery is a wife's equivalent of her husband's wastefulness, both defined as indiscriminate liberality.

We have already seen the association, in the prodigal son story and in its refashioning in the *Henry IV* plays, between the prodigal's carousing among his companions and his evasion of the obligations of marriage; this is the liberality that Bassanio must learn to curb. "These be the Christian husbands," scoffs the miserly Shylock upon hearing Bassanio's and Graziano's offers to sacrifice their wives. Now that Bassanio is entering into wedded life, he needs to acquire a little of Shylock's wary retentiveness, even when so doing conflicts directly with the openhandedness demanded of the friend.[15] The virtue required of him in marriage is the capacity to look to the morrow, to keep futurity in mind because it is tied up with his procreative capacity and with the thriving of the children he hopes to beget. That does not mean Bassanio needs to renounce his friends, but only that his liberality must become more nuanced and more calculating.

In other words, Portia, on the verge of yielding all her authority over her future to Bassanio, urgently needs to clue him in to the necessity of "husbandry," of the wise use of resources, which ipso facto means the denial of some competing claims. The real danger, in *The Merchant of Venice* as in *Timon of Athens,* is not the greedy self-seeking that critics so often darkly want to attribute to the Christians as a group, but rather a wasteful and potentially self-injuring refusal to attend to self-interest. Indeed, the programmatic commitment of Christianity to generosity, especially within the community of believers, means that *any* attention to self-interest, or to future prospects, might be construed as dishonorable or "hypocritical." One cannot reserve things for oneself, but at the same time, one must reserve things for oneself; the property demands upon the "Christian husband" seem to be flatly at odds. In practical terms, fortunately, Portia need not resolve the contradiction, but has only to modify Bassanio's boundless liberality in the direction of greater prudence, for the sake of herself and her future offspring. Whereas for Prince Hal in *Henry IV Part 2* the accession to the throne and the casting off of his prodigal ways require the banishment of the friend, for the now-wealthy private citizen Bassanio, the alternatives are not necessarily so stark.

The difference between the two resolutions is, I think, a generic one. In the *Henry IV* plays, conflicts are resolved by folding them into one marvelously, even implausibly, successful character: Hal simultaneously embodies the normally incompatible roles of prodigal and saver, hero and scapegrace, older son and younger son, aimless picaro and ambitious careerist. In *The Merchant of Venice,* the resolution of conflict does not reside in character but in the imagined environment of the play. The world of Belmont seems so abundant that there is enough for all, and therefore liberality and prudence may both be manifested at once.

And yet, of course, at the end of *The Merchant of Venice* one of the play's most powerful figures is absent. Shylock is formally incorporated into the Christian community by his forced conversion, but excluded from the reunion at Belmont. Shylock's non-presence should point us, I think, to what is being fudged in the tying up of loose ends that the play's conclusion represents. As we have seen, individuals and couples on their own in *The Merchant of Venice* do not suffice, but must look elsewhere for the resources they need. The recipients of these resources, the darlings of fortune, cherish the notion that these resources do not become theirs by depriving others, but instead materialize as if anew from a mysterious source. Informed that he is Shylock's heir, Lorenzo exclaims to Portia and Nerissa: "Fair ladies, you drop manna in the way | Of starved people" (5.1.293–4). And yet, of course, whereas manna is miraculously created from nothing each day as sustenance to God's chosen people, the "manna" that will sustain Lorenzo and Jessica is not the Lord's plenty, much less the provision of Portia and Nerissa, but funds legally wrested from the reluctant Shylock.

The Jew is both the source of fortune and its scapegoat: throughout the play, as C. L. Barber argued in a classic essay, he has championed and represented a principle of scarcity that is momentarily invisible to those presently enjoying Belmont's abundance.[16] The question—and it is a question around which much of the critical debate about *The Merchant of Venice* swirls—is whether that origin ironizes the plenitude, shows it up as chimerical or at least blemished by unjust appropriation, or whether, by contrast, the harmony of the conclusion allegorizes material wealth as moral happiness.

The clashes among the several models of property and relationship in *The Merchant of Venice* produce a yearning for something extra or excess, something "outside the system," that might supplement the insufficiencies of the community without depriving anyone or undermining the integrity of the relationships within it. Here a comparison with the satiric comedies of Ben Jonson helps clarify the issues involved. In, for example, *The Alchemist* or *Volpone*, characters dream of a positive personal transformation that, they imagine, will attend access to miraculous wealth. Yet the plays demonstrate that this fantasy is a ridiculous delusion which only opens up its adherents to victimization. The plain truth, in a Jonson comedy, is that matter cannot be multiplied, that the total amount of wealth in the system is a fixed quantity, and that therefore the only way to accumulate it is to annex it from other claimants. In fact, that unjust seizure is what makes wealth so thrilling for those who possess it or imagine themselves doing so. Volpone shows Celia "a diamond would have bought Lollia Paulina | When she came in starlight, hid with jewels | That were the spoil of provinces" (3.7.194–6) The pillaged provinces make Lollia Paulina's jewels all the more gorgeous; and Volpone's diamond scintillates the more brilliantly insofar as

Volpone imagines it trumping even the vast despoliations of the later Roman empire.[17]

In *The Merchant of Venice*, things are neither so rapacious nor so straightforward. When Antonio stands surety for Bassanio he models the way friends in a community may support one another by making up for one another's lack. Portia does the same when she comes to Antonio's aid in the Venetian courtroom, helping him when he is unable to help himself. While usurious lending or cuckoldry imagine human beings as fungible in a destructive sense, in these cases, one person renders aid to, or stands in the place of, another out of constructive and charitable motives, honoring the relationship between them rather than preying upon it. These rescues strategically rearrange the resources of a larger system so as to confer benefits on a deserving individual who happens, at least at the moment, to lack them. Through such manifold relationships of debt and credit, the community's wealth can be deployed at maximum efficiency even though its total wealth may be limited.

Yet hovering beyond these local adjustments, the play also suggests a more profound supplementation, a more radical form of "standing surety" for others that comes, miraculously, from outside the system and thereby changes the rules by which the system had seemed to operate. That extra may be understood in theological terms as grace or manna or mercy or the music of the spheres, all things which we do not earn or deserve but which are bestowed upon us nonetheless. It may also be figured in natural terms as rain, in narrative terms as inexplicable or unexpected luck, in literary terms as the "happy ending" of comic form.

In Christianity, atonement works by injecting the god-man Christ into what is originally a bilateral transaction between God and fallen mankind, redeeming what had seemed to be a hopelessly unpayable debt. The ease with which the conclusion of *The Merchant of Venice* can be conflated or confused with atonement has received a great deal of attention from critics. And yet a structural similarity is not necessarily an ethical similarity. Antonio may, as C. L. Barber or Barbara Lewalski point out, be construed as a blameless Christ-figure,[18] but at the same time, he describes himself as "a tainted wether of the flock" (4.1.113), and Shakespeare does not gloss over his malignant treatment of Shylock. The merchant and the Jew are both scapegoats, both simultaneously innocent and guilty. Throughout the play a yearning for the transcendence of limit—the poetry of infinite abundance, of wealth swirling on the water, of ineffably beautiful music of the spheres—is countered by a falling short, what Lorenzo calls "this muddy vesture of decay" (5.1.63). And this urgent but thwarted yearning for transcendence is a consequence of the vexed relationship between material and spiritual goods in the Christian tradition—in which, on one hand, a parable can represent a spiritual gift as a sum of money, a "talent," and, on the other hand, the workings of spirit defy the principles of economics.

Notes

1 For a discussion of Shakespeare's likely debt to Aristotle, see Isabella Wheater's two-part essay, "Aristotelian Wealth and the Sea of Love: Shakespeare's Synthesis of Greek Philosophy and Roman Poetry in *The Merchant of Venice*," *Review of English Studies* New Series 43 (1992): 467–87 and 44 (1993): 16–36.

2 The emphasis in friendship theory upon spiritual affinity and upon chosen affiliation produces, Laurie Shannon argues, a utopian paradigm of non-coerced, non-hierarchical obligation that becomes the precursor of the modern liberal subject. Laurie Shannon, *Sovereign Amity: Figures of Friendship in Shakespearean Contexts* (Chicago, IL: University of Chicago Press, 2002).

3 Alan Bray, *The Friend* (Chicago, IL: University of Chicago Press, 2003), p. 115.

4 Bray, pp. 84–139.

5 Craig Muldrew, *The Economy of Obligation: The Culture of Credit and Social Relations in Early Modern England* (London: Palgrave Macmillan), 1998.

6 Francis Bacon, *The Essays or Counsels, Civill and Morall*, ed. Michael Kiernan (Oxford: Clarendon Press, 1985), p. 32.

7 Lars Engle, in *Shakespearean Pragmatism: Market of his Time* (Chicago, IL: University of Chicago Press, 1993), p. 82, remarks of Antonio's "tendency to make financial arrangements personal ones;" in fact this tendency seems shared by everybody in the play.

8 Henry S. Turner, "The Problem of the More-Than-One: Friendship, Calculation, and Political Association in *The Merchant of Venice*," *Shakespeare Quarterly* 57 (2006): 413–42 (439).

9 W. H. Auden, "Brothers and Others," in *The Dyer's Hand and Other Essays* (New York: Random House, 1962), pp. 221–34 (pp. 233–4). Cf. also Alan Sinfield, "It is to contest Antonio's status as lover that Portia...demands of Bassanio the ring which she had given him in her role as wife." ("How to Read *The Merchant of Venice* Without Being Het-

erosexist," in Terence Hawkes, ed., *Alternative Shakespeares*, ii (London: Routledge, 1996), pp. 122–39 (p. 127).)

10 Sinfield, pp. 127–8.

11 See, for instance, Harry Berger, "Marriage and Mercifixion in *The Merchant of Venice*," *Shakespeare Quarterly* 32 (1981): 155–62.

12 See, for instance, Alan Bray, *Homosexuality in Renaissance England* (London: Gay Men's Press, 1982) and *The Friend*.

13 For a discussion of gift exchange more generally in *The Merchant of Venice*, see Ronald A. Sharp, "Gift Exchange and the Economies of Spirit in The Merchant of Venice," *Modern Philology* 83 (1986): 250–65.

14 Laurie Shannon, "Likenings: Rhetorical Husbandries and Portia's 'True Conceit' of Friendship," *Renaissance Drama* New Series 31 (2002): 3–26 (3).

15 Lorna Hutson, *The Usurer's Daughter* (London: Routledge, 1994), pp. 19–23, argues that what, in early modern treatises of household management, often seems to be boringly clichéd advice about frugality was in fact controversial and difficult to implement by its original readers, because it conflicted with a perceived demand for liberality among neighbors.

16 C. L. Barber, "The Merchants and the Jew of Venice: Wealth's Communion and an Intruder," in *Shakespeare's Festive Comedy: A Study of Dramatic Form and its Relation to Social Custom* (Princeton, NJ: Princeton University Press, 1959), pp. 166–91.

17 I make this argument at greater length and in more detail in "Satiric and Ideal Economies in the Jonsonian Imagination," *English Literary Renaissance* 19 (1989): 42–64.

18 Barbara Lewalski, "Biblical Allusion and Allegory in *The Merchant of Venice*," *Shakespeare Quarterly* 13 (1962): 327–43.

5

Vagabond Kings: Entitlement and Distribution in *2 Henry VI* and *King Lear*

I

> "Looking back to discover the genesis of property rights, one necessarily arrives at usurpation. Theft is only punished because it violates the right of property, but this right itself originates in nothing but theft."

> Marquis de Sade, *L'Histoire de Juliette*

In *Richard II*, when the king seizes Bolingbroke's estate, and the Duke of York is wavering whether to support Bolingbroke's rebellion or Richard's right to rule, Bolingbroke presses his sense of grievance:

> Will you permit that I shall stand condemned
> A wandering vagabond, my rights and royalties
> Plucked from my arms perforce?
>
> (2.3.118–20)

Formerly heir apparent to one of the kingdom's wealthiest and most powerful men, now Bolingbroke has lost all the "rights and royalties" that attach to his presumptive position as Duke of Lancaster. And the deprivation has occurred not by process of law but "perforce," merely by Richard's arbitrary exercise of power. The confiscation seems so utterly outrageous that it provokes, as we have seen, a reaction that had earlier seemed impossible, an armed rebellion against a legitimate monarch.

Bolingbroke had already been "wandering" in a legally-imposed six-year exile, but it is specifically the seizure of his property that renders him a "vagabond," someone without a tie to a place. The term was highly charged. Vagrancy was "perhaps the most intractable social problem of the period," as historian A. L. Beier remarks, and "it was in the later sixteenth and early seventeenth centuries that it reached its most menacing proportions."[1] As a rise in population collided with changes in agricultural practice that reduced the demand for labor, internal migration within England and Wales dramatically increased, as large numbers of the poor travelled increasing distances in search of employment or alms. Yet the early modern system of poor relief was administered at the level of the parish; it assumed that indigent persons had a fixed abode and that their welfare was primarily the concern of their immediate neighbors. No one wanted to be taxed to support somebody else's beggars. In this system, the "wandering vagabond" fit in nowhere; he or she was commonly perceived as, and sometimes actually presented, a threat to the settled population. The typical punishment for vagrancy was therefore a form of violent repatriation. The constable tied the vagabond to the tail of a cart and whipped him (or her) around town until bloody, and then issued a passport that permitted him to return to his place of origin—even though he often had none:

> Tramping the roads was a permanent condition for most vagrants. They reported having "small dwelling" and "no abiding place"....When pressed by magistrates, they might produce places of birth or previous residence, but in reality few had regular abodes....Many had been cut loose for years, some for periods exceeding a decade.[2]

In other words, the punishment for vagrancy seems to have willfully ignored reality, insisting against the evidence that everyone had a home and ought to remain there. At the same time the vagabond's separation from the ties of family or from a supervising community rendered him a figure of considerable allure. The "rogue literature" of the period interprets the vagabond's rootlessness as merry liberty, celebrating his clever shifts and his shamelessly improvisatory sexual arrangements.

Bolingbroke presents the annihilation of his right to property and title as scandalous, unthinkable. Yet versions of it are staged again

and again in Shakespeare's plays, from his earliest history plays and
comedies to the late romances, scattered as they are with scions of
royal and noble houses blocked from their birthright. (Needless to
say, none of the real-life vagrants that roamed Elizabethan and
Jacobean England were unaccountably misplaced aristocrats.) Sometimes Shakespeare stages the "romantic" aspects of vagabond life.
For instance, in *The Two Gentlemen of Verona* Valentine is made king
of the outlaws, all of whom turn out to be not ordinary robbers but
gentlemen who have committed crimes of passion in their home
towns. In some of Shakespeare's plays, however, the figure of a royal
or noble "vagabond," theoretically entitled but actually dispossessed,
becomes a way of asking fundamental questions about property relations and social organization.

An early example is what may have been Shakespeare's first history play, *The First Part of the Contention*, otherwise known as *2 Henry
VI*. In its opening scene, a number of Henry's courtiers express
consternation over the terms of the marriage treaty the Earl of Suf-
folk has negotiated on the king's behalf. The agreement requires
Henry to relinquish Anjou and Maine, territories in France that the
English had only recently conquered. This condition so dismays the
Duke of Gloucester, Lord Protector of England, that he is unable to
read the document aloud. The Earl of Warwick, who led the troops
that captured the two provinces, weeps and curses. The Duke of
York points out that England's kings normally demand a dowry
with their wives, rather than paying one.

Yet after the rest of the courtiers depart, York, in a long soliloquy,
voices a different objection to the treaty than the one he had expressed
in company.

> The peers agreed, and Henry was well pleased
> To change two dukedoms for a duke's fair daughter.
> I cannot blame them all—what is't to them?
> 'Tis thine they give away and not their own!
> Pirates may make cheap pennyworths of their pillage,
> And purchase friends, and give to courtesans,
> Still reveling like lords till all be gone,
> Whileas the seely owner of the goods
> Weeps over them, and wrings his hapless hands,

And shakes his head, and, trembling, stands aloof
While all is shared and all is borne away,
Ready to starve and dare not touch his own.
So York must sit and fret and bite his tongue,
While his own lands are bargained for and sold.

(1.2.213–30)

As heir of Edmund Mortimer, next of blood to Richard II, York considers himself the rightful king of England, and Henry VI a usurper. Moreover, he imagines the monarchy as a form of property right—a conception that, as we have already seen, Shakespeare will develop in more detail a few years later when he writes *Richard II*. Barred access to what he calls "his own," York compares himself to a merchant seaman whose goods have been seized by pirates. Ignoring the other courtiers' political and strategic objections to Henry VI's marriage treaty, and discounting as well his own considerable wealth, power, and status, York sees himself self-pityingly as an isolated victim, "hapless" and "seely," without redress.

In the *Henry VI* plays, the House of York has the superior pedigree, but the House of Lancaster has de facto possession of the crown. The separation of these normally coexistent but conceptually distinct forms of entitlement leads to an impasse, and as a result the property rules that are supposed to preserve tranquility instead lead to violence. And once conflict is joined, each side produces a narrative of events that construes itself as the rightful owner, and the opponent as the "pirate": wild, unscrupulous, dangerously mobile, entirely outside the settled social order. In this self-justifying story, however, the pirate—a "vagabond" at the beginning of the story—with shocking disregard for propriety, seizes the goods and displaces their rightful owner. At that point the dispossessed party has two options: he can impotently acquiesce, or he can become a pirate himself, seeking revenge and restitution.

The difference York draws between the rightful owner of property and the pirate who steals and wastes it thus tends to be unstable in plot terms, with the "rightful owner" and the "pirate" liable suddenly to switch places. It is unstable ethically as well. Despite their incompatible property claims, the rival parties always appeal to inheritance and to custom, rehearsing their grievance as a chronicle of rightful possession followed by real or threatened robbery by an interloper. This harking back to the past is critical because the "right of first possession" is deeply ingrained in law and practice, and is perhaps fundamental to intuitions about what constitutes a property claim: the strongest title is assumed to be the oldest. Unfortunately, the apparent inevitability of anyone's "first possession" tends to disappear once the temporal context is sufficiently enlarged. As Francis Bacon writes: "Those that are first raised to nobility are commonly more virtuous, but less innocent, than their descendants; for there is rarely any rising but by a commixture of good and evil arts."[3] When the origins of titles are closely scrutinized, this "commixture" tends to become embarrassingly obvious. It was common knowledge in Shakespeare's time that existing land tenures in England had been abolished and then reinstituted from scratch by William I in the years following the Norman Conquest, enriching William's French associates at the expense of native landholders. In 1276 the common-law courts therefore stipulated that the phrase "from time immemorial" was a term of art that actually meant "since 1189," the earliest date at which property claims were allowed to be legally substantiated. As a practical matter, however, given the imperfections of the written record, even this relatively modest definition of "immemoriability" presented difficulties in adjudicating rival property claims, resulting in what legal historian A. W. B. Simpson calls an "extraordinarily complex body of law."[4] Shortening the period required to establish a claim to property seemed to offer a partial remedy. By the reign of Henry VIII, a mere thirty to sixty years of uncontested possession, depending upon the kind of title involved, sufficed to establish an "immemorial" entitlement, a legal principle still preserved in the English and American doctrine of adverse possession. But in sustaining the right of the interloper in the interests of maintaining the status quo, this doctrine contradicts the right of first possession, or at least limits the circumstances in which that right can be asserted.

In other words, a title to property that purports to originate in the misty reaches of time is very likely to be merely a theft that has aged. Although the immediate scandal may have faded, and although the legal system may find it practical to prohibit challenges to possession after a certain period of time, it is hard to see that the passage of years alters the propriety of the original seizure. "What in me was purchased | Falls upon thee in a more fairer sort," the dying Henry IV reassures his son, "so thou the garland wear'st successively" (*2 Henry IV* 4.3.328–30). But he nonetheless advises the prince that "thou art not firm enough," and Henry V will continue to worry, on the eve of the Battle of Agincourt, that God may remain inclined to punish him for his father's misdeeds: "Not today, O Lord, | O not today, think not upon the fault | My father made in compassing the crown" (*Henry V* 4.1.274–6). God's justice, slow but sure, is not subject to the time limits set by common law.

The pirate and proprietor, the landowner and vagrant, are thus both contraries to and replicas of one another. As the Marquis de Sade notes in the epigram to this chapter, while proprietary right seems theft's opposite, it is arguably merely theft's institutionalization. This is especially the case for kings and the upper aristocracy, whose seizures are often glorified as conquest, supposedly the highest achievement of powerful men.

The Second Part of the Contention repeatedly stages encounters between the most richly entitled persons in the realm and its marginal or dispossessed members: encounters that figure their violent collision as an uncanny doubling. The effect is particularly marked in the episodes treating the Cade rebellion, as Ronald Knowles points out: "Where at one moment we respond to inversion, distortion, and burlesque, at another we find they have become a version, reflection, and duplication."[5] We first hear of Jack Cade from York, who reports that Cade proved himself a tough and resourceful soldier in Ireland, so similar to the wild Irish that he could conduct espionage concealed as one of them. Yet he also closely resembles John Mortimer, the recently-deceased rightful heir to the throne of England, "in face, in gait, in speech" (3.1.73). Cade is thus simultaneously indistinguishable from the enemy outsider and from an ultimate insider. Likewise the movement he leads simultaneously erupts "from below" and is directed in secret "from above," by the second person in the realm.

When Cade finally appears, the dialogue calls attention to his paradoxical juxtaposition of extremes. "My father was a Mortimer," Cade declaims, apparently following a script provided him by York, "My mother a Plantagenet...my wife descended of the Lacys"

(4.2.33–8). Whereas, in other contexts, Shakespeare brings onto the stage princes and earls who have been reduced to vagabondage, here Cade himself fraudulently seizes the role of the vagabond-king, positioning himself as if he were the character in a romance, the son of a royal child stolen by a beggar-woman. Yet while he boasts, his follower the Butcher ridicules this account in a counterpoint of asides: Cade's father "had never a house but a cage"; his mother gave birth to him under a hedge; his wife is a tramp. Cade himself, according to the Butcher, has been "whipped three market days altogether," the common punishment for vagrancy. Elsewhere in the play, Cade is described as a cloth-worker and the son of a brick-layer: of an artisan background, in other words, but hardly a home-less vagrant. The Butcher's denigration of Cade is perhaps thus as fictionally extravagant as Cade's self-elevation: acclaim seems to call forth slander.

As many critics have noticed, Cade's willful brutality, however appalling, differs little from the behavior of the aristocratic thugs in *2 Henry VI*. "The larger context for his grim saturnalia of violence," writes Jean Howard in her introduction to the play in *The Norton Shakespeare*, "is the unspeakable selfishness of the English nobles."[6] In a world in which all property claims seem patently to be thefts and counter-thefts, the contemptuous ambition of the high and the re-sentful envy of the low come to the same thing: untrammeled homi-cidal ferocity, instanced by a relentless train of summary hangings and headings. Shakespeare's version of the Cade rebellion ties this violence directly to disputes over property. He departs from his sources to incorporate elements of several different popular rebel-lions: Wat Tyler's Peasant's Revolt in the reign of Richard II, and various sixteenth century insurrections—Jan Leiden's uprising in Germany, the Kett Revolt in Norfolk, and a series of riots in London. While the historical Cade's grievances were largely political and his party included Kentish landholders as well as peasants, artisans, and shopkeepers, Shakespeare's Cade voices the economic and status resentments of the lower orders, and outlines a program of radical social and economic leveling. Private property and the use of money will be eliminated, along with institutions such as the law courts and the schools that have enforced those distinctions. As Shakespeare presents it, Cade's revolt, in all its comic, carnivalian grotesquerie and excess, makes the question "who should rule?" into a question about the distribution of wealth: "Who gets what?"

Whereas Henry VI traces his title back to his father and grandfather, and Richard Duke of York goes back one more generation to challenge the Lancastrian claim, Cade's rebels open up an indefinite temporal vista. "It was never merry world in England since gentlemen came up," opines one of Cade's followers, evoking a distant golden age of social equality. When Stafford reminds Cade of his low origins—"Thy father was a plasterer | And thou thyself a shearman, art thou not?"—Cade replies, "And Adam was a gardener" (4.2.121–3). Originally, all men labored with their hands, and there was no distinction between gentleman and commoner. The cogency of the artisans' position is hard to refute. Yet in practice, the evocation of an indefinitely long past ironically does not enhance but annihilates history, and with it the restraints upon tyranny imposed by a respect for that history. "Burn all the records of the realm," orders Cade; "My mouth shall be the Parliament of England" (4.7.13–14). The tension between the law of first possession, which honors precedent and ties ownership to antiquity, and the law of adverse possession, which favors the maintenance of a status quo possibly based upon unjust seizure, is here stretched well past the breaking point.

As mayhem swirls though the entire realm, the estate of the Kentish esquire Alexander Iden seems, at first, a miraculous island of tranquility. It is described as a garden surrounded by the obvious boundary of a brick wall. "Lord, who would live turmoiléd in the court | And may enjoy such quiet walks as these?" Iden wonders.

> This small inheritance my father left me
> Contenteth me, and worth a monarchy.
> I seek not to wax great by others waning,
> Or gather wealth I care not with what envy:
> Sufficeth that I have maintains my state,
> And sends the poor well pleased from my gate.
>
> (4.9.16–21)

Here again Shakespeare deviates from his sources. The historical Iden was a sheriff who pursued the fugitive Cade to the town of

Heathfield, in Sussex, after Henry VI revoked a previously-issued pardon. In Shakespeare's reimagining, Iden represents a middle term between the starkly polarized, yet uncannily mirroring, opposites of high and low: a "lord of the soil" from the perspective of the starving, hunted Cade, Alexander Iden is the proprietor of a mere "small inheritance" from an aristocratic point of view. His walled garden seems to give the lie to Cade's communist fantasy, exemplifying the security that landed property is supposed to underwrite. Iden is protected against misery by resources of his own soil, and from the gusts of political fortune at court by his ability to withdraw into a clearly demarcated private refuge. For peers of the realm, as we have already seen, claims to land are the basis of significant political authority; but for the same reason, those claims are precarious, since ambitious rivals have a strong motive to seek to overturn them. In this system, the most secure property rights seem to be those of the moderately prosperous. So although Iden believes his "small inheritance" is "worth a monarchy," given what we see elsewhere in the play it is arguably worth even more, since England's monarchs or pretenders to monarchy seem never to enjoy the tranquil luxury of Iden's unchallenged possession.

It is from the point of view of the middling sort, moreover, that the similarities between the high and the low become most apparent. The king and upper nobility, with their widespread landholdings, resemble the vagabond in that they are relatively unfettered to a particular location. A lack of rootedness encourages both the very powerful and the entirely disempowered to cast off the discipline imposed by membership in a small, close-knit community, as embodied in the law. Instead both the very rich and the very poor pursue their own self-preservation or self-promotion without regard to the well-being of others. Thus the openly adulterous Queen Margaret and Sussex respect the bonds of marriage no more than does Cade's reputedly sluttish wife, or his follower the Butcher, who commits rape with impunity. Iden, by contrast, tied closely to a place, lacks the wherewithal to mount a power-grab, yet does not suffer the poverty that incites the lowest in society to crime. Because he has something to lose, it is in his interest to keep his behavior within bounds. He and his kind are thus effectively constrained by

the law, and at the same time encouraged by modest incentives to
support the established order.

Iden's security, then, is dependent upon a limitation—perhaps a
deliberate demarcation—of scope, as clear as the brick wall around
his garden. Just as his estate covers a small geographic area, his temporal range is restricted too: while the Duke of York chafes at an
injustice committed several generations back, it suffices Iden that he
knows he inherited from his father. This myopia is vividly clear onstage, for even as Iden declaims sententiously of his "quiet walks" he
comically fails to notice that his garden is already occupied. His
complacency can be disrupted from below by a belligerent invader;
it can be disrupted from above by the favor of a king who demands
that the "hero" henceforth attend him at court. The inviolability of
property seems, at best, not a natural right but an expedient fiction.

A great deal of ink has been spilled on Shakespeare's political
commitments in *2 Henry VI*. Among recent critics, Stephen Greenblatt
and Richard Helgerson consider him murderously hostile toward
the commoner rebels, while Annabel Patterson and Tom Cartelli
argue for a more sympathetic engagement with populist sentiment.[7]
Perhaps the problem is that much of the rhetoric of the play suggests a bipartite conflict between the "noble" and "base" with nothing in between. Yet Iden seems to embody the possibility of a third,
interposing term. When, in the late 1590s, Shakespeare began to
wax prosperous, he set himself up in a situation very similar to the
one he delineates for Iden; he purchased New Place in Stratford,
and eventually occupied a thriving but not grand position as a
small-scale provincial landholder. Thus for the young Shakespeare,
his largely fictional Iden may have embodied a personal aspiration.
And the sense of discrimination both from the very rich and the
very poor may structure not only Shakespeare's ultimate ambitions
but his self-conception as an actor and playwright even at the outset
of his career. Richard Helgerson has remarked on the way the script
of *The First Part of the Contention* prescribes that actors, themselves
of artisan background, continually hurl insults at Cade and his
supporters.

> How do we account for the fact that this play, so thickly
> crammed with class slurs, was written, played, and viewed by

base, abject, ignoble villains, grooms, and clowns? Did none of them notice that they were themselves the objects of the abuse they were so generously handing out?...Or was their point...that their very participation in this rite of flouting vaccinated them?...If so, it must have been an uncomfortable and unstable exemption.[8]

For Helgerson, this is a case of the pot calling the kettle black; after all, the 1572 Statute of Vagabonds specifies in its list of undesirables the "common players of interludes." What Helgerson misses, perhaps, is that the Statute of Vagabonds, by excepting "players of interludes belonging to any baron of the realm," has the effect of *differentiating* Shakespeare and his fellows from the itinerant actors. In other words, the statute grants the established, patronized theater companies a legal monopoly on entertainment by blocking competition from unauthorized talent. In comparison to an aristocratic man of leisure, indeed, Shakespeare may feel himself cheated of fortune, his name "branded" by a scandalous profession, his nature "almost subdued | To what it works in, like the dyer's hand" (sonnet 111). But at the same time Shakespeare and his associates, with their noble patron, their valuable real and chattel property, and their increasingly bountiful stream of income, could well have conceived themselves, as Iden does, on the side of privilege, not on the side of deprivation. In that case they would not consider themselves "the objects of the abuse they were so generously handing out," but as proudly exempt from that abuse. Nonetheless, given that Shakespeare draws attention to the ironies of Iden's situation, it seems unlikely that he was blind to his own.

The conflicts over property rights in *2 Henry VI* are, most of the time, questions of entitlement: who has the best, in the sense of most unassailable and legally sound, claim to England? Yet there is another way of thinking about property that surfaces occasionally in the play: a register not of solace or ambition but of desperate bodily urgency. What is to Iden a bucolic retreat that anchors him to his familial past, is for Cade a place to "eat grass or pick a sallet" (4.9.7). He trespasses upon Iden's grounds not because he wants to make a statement about private property rights but merely because he is ravenous. The stage direction specifies that Cade lies prone, "picking of herbs," almost an animal at pasture: an association strengthened when Cade refers to himself as a "stray," a escaped bullock that could be impounded by the person whose land he grazed upon. For his part, Iden sees his responsibility as small land-holder as entailing the relief of beggars—he "sends the poor well pleased from my gate," he claims (4.9.21)—and even when Cade belligerently accosts him, he is at first reluctant to fight with "a poor famished man." Yet whereas the deference of the beggars flatters and reinforces Iden's proprietary role—by petitioning at his *gate* they acknowledge his control over access to his land—Cade's headlong presumption offends against it. Leaping over the wall and eating Iden's vegetables without permission, Cade alters what the provision of food means: not a matter of the proprietor's beneficence but of the vagabond's unceremonious demand. Cade's aggressive speech exacerbates his offense, as Iden incredulously remarks.

> Is't not enough to break into my garden,
> And, like a thief, to come to rob my grounds,
> Climbing my walls in spite of me the owner,
> But thou wilt brave me with these saucy terms?
>
> (4.9.30–3)

One of the ironies of the scene is that Iden does not recognize the fugitive and is inclined at first to pity his sorry state, so that if Cade had politely asked for relief without identifying himself he might well have received succor. Instead, too hungry to be deferential, Cade invites his own death.

Cade's plight echoes an episode earlier in the play, when the poor, apparently disabled Simpcox claims to have miraculously re-gained his sight at the shrine of St Alban's. Unlike the gullible King Henry, the Duke of Gloucester immediately realizes that Simpcox is a fake, and exposes him with a few pointed questions. He then pro-nounces sentence on Simpcox and his wife: "Let them be whipped through every market-town | Till they come to Berwick, from whence they came" (2.1.158–9). This is the punishment routinely meted out in early modern England to vagabonds and "sturdy beggars" who have departed from their home towns, hoping to take advan-tage of the kindness of strangers. The general tenor of the scene, not to mention the play as a whole, establishes Gloucester as a wise judge, indeed the ethical center of the play. Yet one line threatens to undermine his moral authority. "Alas, sir," cries Simpcox's wife, as the beadle hauls her off to be flogged, "We did it for pure need" (2.1.157). Gloucester's investigative acumen, directed to discovering a punishable "truth," simply passes over, as legally negligible, the Simpcox couple's motives for dissimulation.

There is a similar moment of incongruity and incomprehension in Act 4 scene 7. After having chastised Lord Saye for having followed the letter of the law in his role as judge, Cade accuses him of adorning his horse with a foot-cloth, a common way to indicate distinction of rank. Like Gloucester, Saye is a sympathetic, intelligent character, and even in Cade's distorted account he seems to have executed his duties conscientiously. But here he fails to get the point: "What of that?" he asks. "Thou ought'st not to let thy horse wear a cloak when honester men than thou go in their hose and doublet," replies Cade (40–2). While Saye considers the footcloth an innocent, even decorous adornment, to Cade it constitutes an outrageous flouting of luxury in the face of others' destitution.

The miscommunication here, and the other similar moments in *2 Henry VI*, point to a rupture or breakdown in the property system. The rules of property prescribe who owns what, and when those rules are violated, an efficient legal system restores the goods to the "proper" owner. Part of the problem in *2 Henry VI*, of course, is that people fail to respect this law, indeed actively undermine it. But another part of the problem is something that the law itself apparently fails to acknowledge. For off to the side, as it were, unaddressed by the rules of entitlement and fair procedure, remain several urgent questions of distributive justice. Should one man starve when another man has plenty to spare in his garden? Should a horse wear a cloak while a man shivers in the cold? Wise judges like Gloucester or Saye are not obliged to address such matters. Yet as a result, just as the right to property relies upon obscuring the truth as much as upon revealing it, so also the law that institutes property can easily seem a fiction designed to maintain the power of the rich at the expense of the poor. In *2 Henry VI*, Shakespeare often seems close to the insights of late twentieth century critical legal scholars, who emphasize the way the law reinforces the power of elites, although he does not apparently share their reformist convictions. While demonstrating that the law of property is inequitable, he also suggests that the only hope for social stability will rest in the recovery of respect for the law. Yet the problem of grossly and inexplicably disproportionate distribution remains, an offense against justice broadly if not narrowly conceived.

II

King Lear does not merely feature one vagabond-king, but swarms with them. All of the virtuous, highborn characters are cut loose from their moorings: Cordelia disinherited, Kent exiled, the King wandering on the heath, the outlawed Edgar disguised as a mad beggar, Gloucester blinded by houseguests and cast out of his home to "smell | His way to Dover" (3.7.96–7). As in *2 Henry VI*, *King Lear* thus combines a conflict over power and entitlement in the uppermost echelon of society with scenes of deprivation among the dispossessed. Yet the effect is not merely to reprise the critique of property in the earlier play, but to suggest an even more radical conclusion. Indeed the effect of *Lear*'s wholesale disjointings is to complicate, almost to the extent of annihilating, the powerful connections between property and power as they have been asserted in many of Shakespeare's other plays.

These connections begin to come under pressure at the outset of the play, when Lear announces the division of his kingdom. What exactly is being conveyed, or promised, in this scene? To whom is it being conveyed? And why is the conveyance happening at this moment?

King Lear takes place in the remote past, in a "Britain" that apparently lacks many of the government institutions familiar in medieval and early modern England, and that are at least cursorily depicted in the chronicle history plays. There is apparently no ecclesiastical hierarchy, no Parliament, and no judicial system; as the play opens Lear's authority is absolute and completely undelegated to others. Yet despite this apparent primitivism, Lear's provision for his daughters is in some ways a routine, "civilized" arrangement. As we have already seen, by English common law an eldest son inherits the bulk of a landed estate in preference to his sisters or his younger brothers, who receive smaller "portions" designed to marry them off or set them up in a profession. In default of male heirs, a daughter might inherit just as an eldest son would, but with some complications for her birth family, as we have already observed in *The Merchant of Venice*. In that play, both Jessica and Portia are only children, and apparently the only blood relations to whom their fathers' property could conceivably flow. In cases where there are no sons but multiple surviving daughters, the principle of primogeniture does not apply; instead landed property is split up equally among the girls, a system called "partible inheritance." Lear follows this pattern, tweaking it to reflect his acknowledged preference for Cordelia. He divides the realm in thirds; the parts allotted to Goneril and Regan are exactly equivalent, so that "curiosity in neither can make choice of either's moiety" (1.1.5–6), while Cordelia's third, presumably the same quantity of territory, is nonetheless "more opulent than your sisters'" (1.2.85). It is the familiarity of this arrangement which leads Richard Strier to argue for the reasonableness of Lear's initial plan, calling it "sensible and politically astute."[9]

As we have seen, *Richard II* and the *Henry IV* plays typically construe sovereignty as a form of property right, and Lear's plan suggests that he, too, takes the disposition of property as a model for the disposition of a realm. Yet the special circumstance in which multiple royal daughters stand to inherit suggests that, in this case, simply conflating *dominium* and *imperium* might be misguided or positively dangerous. Lear's stated aim is "to publish | Our daughters' several dowers, that future strife | May be prevented now" (1.1.42–3). Yet he fails to anticipate that his action will not forestall but rather will foment political crisis. Partible inheritance, reasonable as it may be for non-royal daughters, imperils the safety of the realm by weakening each individual ruler without indicating a hierarchy among them. Indeed, as soon as Goneril and Regan inherit—before they begin struggling over Edmund, and when they are still colluding against their father—rumors begin to mount of civil war between them, and of an invasion by the forces of Cordelia.

In sixteenth-century England, the "excess daughters" problem was no mere theoretical concern. In the reigns of Henry VIII and Edward VI, three Parliamentary Succession Acts in 1533, 1536, and 1544, and a royal "devise" in 1553, each attempt to determine the order of inheritance among female claimants to the English throne: Mary Tudor, Elizabeth Tudor, and Lady Jane Grey. The shifting terms of these documents, settling the kingdom on first one, then another, then another, do not merely reflect the uncharted waters into which Henry's marital adventures had launched his realm. They also suggest that, compared to the clear-cut "rightness" of succession by the king's eldest son, the entitlements of royal daughters were uncertain. Still, despite a lack of consensus as to who, exactly, the heir might be, the various Henrician and Edwardian attempts to settle the succession never envisage splitting the realm into pieces. Instead they preserve the kingdom's integrity by ordering the daughters in a "succession queue."

In Lear's particular family circumstances, the fact that two of his daughters are already married raises a further problem: the question of to whom the segmented realm is actually being conveyed. Lear begins the love-test by addressing Albany and Cornwall, and calling the kingdom he means to divide "our daughters' several dowers." In other words, he apparently assumes that the daughters' entitlement will pass to their husbands "under coverture," as property normally would in marriage, and therefore invests the husbands, not his daughters, with "my power, | Preeminence, and all the large effects | That troop with majesty" (130–2). This is the assumption of Kent and Gloucester as well in the opening lines of the play:

> KENT   I thought the king had more affected the Duke of
>   Albany than Cornwall.
> GLOUCESTER   It did always seem so to us: but now, in
>   the division of the kingdom it appears not which of the
>   dukes he values most.
>
> (1.1.1–5)

Kent and Gloucester speculate about the king's attitude toward Albany and Cornwall because they assume that the husbands of Goneril and Regan will be the de facto recipients of any territories granted to their wives. And although—unlike Hotspur, Glendower, and Mortimer in *1 Henry IV*—Lear does not verbally specify the geographical boundaries of his daughters' allotments, the play does imply that his segmentation of his kingdom takes their husbands' native origins into account. Cornwall is in the west of England, as is Gloucestershire; since the Duke of Gloucester refers to Cornwall as "my master, | My worthy arch and patron" (2.1.59–60), it is reasonable to surmise that Regan's land is located in the west. Albany is in what, for Shakespeare, would have been Scotland—so Goneril's third of the kingdom is presumably its northern lands. Cordelia, with two suitors from the Continent, would in the original disposition of the realm have likely received the fertile and populous southeast, including, perhaps not coincidentally, the ancestral base of her loyal supporter Kent. This "dower" would not only amount to "a third more opulent than your sisters" but would be conveniently accessible for either of Cordelia's Continental suitors.

Whether or not these speculations are reasonable, it is still unclear if a regnant queen's husband—a son-in-law rather than a "son of the blood"—is really a king in every respect. Prior to the marriage of Queen Mary to Philip of Spain in 1554, Parliament carefully delineated his role; he was to be called "King," but he did not acquire the powers Mary's half-brother Prince Edward would have possessed had he survived to maturity. Philip reigned not in his own person but jointly with his wife and only during her lifetime, and was depicted together with her on coins of the realm. All documents needed both the king's and the queen's signature. Moreover Philip was specifically denied certain prerogatives: for instance, he could not muster men for foreign wars. In 1579–80, the prospect of Elizabeth I's marriage to the Duke of Anjou raised similar concerns, pitting strongly held convictions about proper wifely subordination against xenophobic worries about the potential power of a foreign ruler. Here is another dilemma that Lear apparently fails to anticipate. Confronted by Albany with proof of her adultery with Edmund, Goneril informs her husband that he has no authority over her: "The laws are mine, not thine" (5.3.157–8). Albany considers this assertion "most monstrous," but Goneril, her monstrousness aside, is possibly correct. Her conviction that via her performance of the love test she has received sovereignty in her own person, not as a conduit to her husband, opens another distinction between property entitlement and sovereignty that had not existed in *Richard II*.

If the challenge for the father without a male heir is to settle his property suitably, giving away both goods and girls, the daughter, for her part, must split her loyalty between father and husband, old and young patriarch. Although Lear divides his realm in a perhaps-unwise but nonetheless familiar way, he does so by means of a bizarre love test that puts an apparently insurmountable roadblock in the way of one daughter's reception of his gift. The love test, as Lynda Boose has pointed out, puts Cordelia in an impossible position.[10] By demanding all of Cordelia's love in order to release her dowry, Lear seems at the same time to disqualify her from marriage— because, as she points out, she needs to reserve some love for her future husband:

> Haply, when I shall wed,
> That lord whose hand must take my plight shall carry
> Half my love with him, half my care and duty.
> Sure, I shall never marry like my sisters,
> To love my father all.

> (1.1.99–103)

Goneril and Regan, Cordelia strongly implies, are either lying about their love for Lear, or do not love their husbands properly; in fact, the play will bear her out in both suspicions. But their prevarications matter little for their status in life since they are already irrevocably married, no matter what they tell their father now. Cordelia's situation is unsettled and so the tenor of her reply has potentially significant consequences. Moreover, as Boose argues, if Cordelia refuses to cooperate, Lear may still hope to retain her, because he assumes that no husband will accept her without a dowry. Heads I win, tails you lose. Cordelia may either dismiss her suitors by pledging her total allegiance to her father, or they may dismiss themselves once they realize that she brings no portion with her. This giving-with-one-hand-while-taking-away-with-another perhaps reflects the unresolved possessiveness of Lear's love for his youngest child.

When Cordelia provokes her father's fury and forfeits her inheritance, however, the action spirals out of Lear's control. And the way it does so speaks both to some of the core issues of this book, and to a central dispute in the *Lear* criticism. Lear's love test bluntly asserts both that a ceremonial declaration suffices as "love," and that a bequest of wealth is the same as, or is completely fungible with, "love." Yet Cordelia's refusal to comply with its terms seems to challenge both these assertions and to insist that "love" is something other, or elsewhere. Stanley Cavell writes:

> This is the way I understand that opening scene with the three daughters. Lear knows that it is a bribe he offers, and—part of him anyway—wants exactly what a bribe can buy: 1) false love and 2) a public expression of love. That is, he wants something he does not have to return *in kind,* something which a division of his property fully pays for...Cordelia is alarming precisely because he knows she is offering the real thing, offering something a more opulent third of his kingdom cannot, must not, repay; putting a claim upon him he cannot face.[11]

In Cavell's reading, shame inhibits Lear from acknowledging his love: shame both at his own vulnerability and excess of feeling, and possibly too, Cavell speculates, at the "*nature* of his love for Cordelia [which is] too far from the plain love of father for daughter." The love test forecloses any need to acknowledge what Cavell regards as Lear's "true feelings," which have nothing to do with a bequest of property. In fact, the realness of "the real thing" is manifested by its distance from such concerns: by the fact that a third of a kingdom "cannot, must not" be fungible with it.

Margreta de Grazia, however, in what seems to be a flatly incompatible reading, asserts that in the "premodern" conceptual world of *Lear*, property and person are inextricable: "removing what a person *has* simultaneously takes away what a person *is*...having is tantamount to being, *not* having is tantamount to *non*-being."[12] For de Grazia, the scandal of the first scene is not that Lear makes a love test the condition for disposing of his realm, but that he believes he can dispose of it at all:

> Lear's initial attempt to disburden himself of his property might...be reconsidered in light of popular and medical lore on insanity...Both plot and subplot dramatize the impossibility of the severing Lear attempts. Persons and things cannot be alienated from one another.

If de Grazia is correct, it is hard to claim that the Lear of the first scene is making a horrible error by confusing love and wealth, because there is no way that "love" could be conceptualized independent of a property entitlement. Instead his horrible error is just the opposite, a lunatic failure to understand that necessarily "as estate clings to person so person clings to estate."[13]

Who is right? I think this issue is less clear-cut than either Cavell or de Grazia allows. The idea that property, love, and social status are deeply implicated in one another is a part of the story as Shakespeare inherits it. In Holinshed, Cordelia tells Lear: "I have loved you ever, and will continually (while I live) as my natural father. And if you would more understand of the love that I bear you, ascertain yourself, that so much as you have, so much you are worth, and so much I love you, and no more."[14] In *The Mirror of Magistrates* she is even blunter, informing Lear that "We love you chiefly for the goods you have." Shakespeare's Cordelia is more ambiguous: "I love your majesty | According to my bond" (1.1.91–2). As we have seen in *The Merchant of Venice*, the word "bond" can refer, often simultaneously, to an emotional commitment, a financial instrument, and a physical constraint, but in any construal the word certainly does not exclude a material component.

The scene as it begins, then, seems to bear out de Grazia's claims, but as it goes on, the Cavell alternative begins to seem more plausible. Lear, in a rage, disinherits Cordelia and calls her suitors before him to inform them of that fact. Throughout early modern Europe royal and aristocratic marriages, of course, were generally undertaken explicitly with a view to political and material advantages. Even in lower social spheres Shakespeare is often matter-of-fact about such motives ("I come to wive it wealthily in Padua," Petruchio remarks insouciantly in *The Taming of the Shrew* (1.2.72); "he that can lay hold of her | Shall have the chinks," says the Nurse of her charge in *Romeo and Juliet* (1.5.113–14)). Thus it is not in the least surprising that Burgundy declines to marry a princess who has just been disinherited. Yet Cordelia expresses gentle contempt for his hesitancy:

> Peace be with Burgundy!
> Since that respects of fortune are his love,
> I shall not be his wife.

> (1.1.248–50)

She implies unmistakably that "respects of fortune" are not the same as "love," though Burgundy may be ignorant of the difference. And the King of France is even more explicit.

> Love's not love
> When it is mingled with regards that stands
> Aloof from th'entire point.

$$(1.1.239–41)$$

For France, Cordelia possesses an intrinsic worth apart from the lands her father might bestow upon her. "She is herself a dowry," he declares, and takes her to wife. Cavell, who as we have seen reads *King Lear* in terms of an absolute distinction between spiritual and material worth, is overjoyed that somebody in the play is making that distinction: he writes of "one's rush of gratitude toward France, one's almost wild relief as he speaks his beautiful trust." Cavell insists upon the importance of casting the small role of France with "an actor of authority and distinction" and fondly recalls a 1946 student production in which the character "was given his full sensitivity and manliness."[15] Meanwhile de Grazia, who argues that the "premodern" imagination is incapable of precisely the differentiation France makes here, simply declines to discuss this passage at all.

The upshot of the scene taken as a whole is therefore double, both emphasizing the self-interested motives for which family members might love one another, and at the same time disowning or deprecating that self-interest. In the next act the Fool sings:

> Fathers that wear rags
> Do make their children blind;
> But fathers that bear bags
> Shall see their children kind.
> Fortune, that arrant whore,
> Ne'er turns the key to the poor.

$$(2.4.46–51)$$

For the Fool, the connection between the father's wealth and the "kindness" of children is simultaneously routine and dishonorable. It is the way of the world, but the way of the world is venal, and Fortune is "an arrant whore." By satirizing covetous love the Fool suggests, like France, that love might also be judged by another standard in which material considerations are "aloof from th'entire point."

The ability of the Fool, France, Kent, or Cordelia to separate love, and the intrinsic worth of loved persons, from their material circumstances appears throughout the play as a form of nobility. So it's worth pointing out that Edmund's first soliloquy in Act 1 scene 2 strangely echoes what Cavell calls the "beautifully disinterested" attitude of the King of France as expressed near the end of the previous scene. Edmund distinguishes "the curiosity of nations," which heaps the family property upon the legitimate child, from "nature," which creates bastards as excellent as their legitimate brethren. "My dimensions are as well compact, | My mind as generous, and my shape as true | As honest madam's issue" (1.2.7–9). Lear loves his daughters unequally, but custom encourages him to make their inheritances more or less equivalent. Gloucester, on the other hand, loves his sons equally, but custom differentiates their inheritance. In both cases, emotional bonds between fathers and children fail to match up with widely accepted conventions of property management. A gap opens between how much a person is loved or loveable, and his fortunes in life, defined by both Edmund and France as that which is "aloof from th'entire point." Yet Edmund's motives for insisting upon that gap are, of course, very different from France's. In other words, it is not the distinction between property and person, fortune and intrinsic worth, that is per se virtuous or vicious, but rather the reasons that distinction is elaborated and the ends for which it is deployed.

As in *Richard II*, the plot of *King Lear* separates the person of the king from the possession of a kingdom, creating conundrums of identity for the dispossessed monarch and crises of loyalty for his erstwhile subjects. Yet while Richard's public yielding up of his throne is in fact organized by the successful usurper, so that his compliance is only nominally voluntary, Lear chooses to give up his kingdom under no apparent duress. In most cases, of course, a king's realm descends to his heir only upon his death, so in a sense, by attempting "to shake all cares and business from our age," Lear is divesting himself prematurely. The rashness of his action is certainly the lesson the Fool will draw: "Thou hadst little wit in thy bald crown, when thou gavest thy golden one away" (1.4.141–2). However, daughters generally, as we saw in *The Merchant of Venice*, tend to make temporally inconvenient demands upon paternal property; their marriages, not the father's death, are the usual occasions on which their portions are paid out. So at least in the case of his elder daughters, Lear's dowry arrangements seem belated rather than premature. In fact the clearest rationale for acting now, rather than either earlier or later, may be the imminent nuptials of Cordelia, whose two suitors, he says, "here are to be answered" (1.1.46). Unlike Cornwall and Albany, Cordelia's suitors are not Lear's subjects, and he must negotiate with them as equals.

Yet surely Lear could have provided for his daughters without abdicating entirely. For whatever reason, Lear believes that he can give up "power, | Pre-eminence, and all the large effects | That troop with majesty" while nonetheless maintaining "all th'addition of a king." By "addition" he means primarily "titles of honor"— Lear wants to be called "King" although he is no longer holding the reins of the state. But the word of course suggests something supernumerary: what can be added can also be subtracted. As soon as Goneril and Regan receive their portions of the kingdom, they begin to remove "th'addition," pouring contempt upon Lear's expectation: "Idle old man, | That still would manage those authorities | That he hath given away" (1.3.16–18). Yet Lear does not really desire or expect to wield the power he has relinquished; he only wants the one hundred retainers he has "reserved" in his original stipulation. In a moment of intense frustration Lear imagines his gift of the realm as a reversible one: "Thou shalt find | That I'll resume the shape which thou dost think | I have cast off for ever; thou shalt, I warrant thee" (1.4.285–7). Yet this desperate counterfactual assertion is only a measure of his actual impotency in the face of his daughters' intransigence.

In a sense Lear, as he is well aware, has made his own uncomfortable bed for himself. By implying that love is a proper response to wealth, Lear's love test suggests that it is right for his daughters to love them because he can give them things. As Holinshed's Cordelia puts it: "so much as you have, so much you are worth, and so much I love you, and no more." But the dark corollary is that the daughters may love him only insofar as he can give them things, opening him up to their abuse as soon as he no longer has the means with which to be liberal.

What, then, does Lear intend to achieve by laying down his power and wealth? As we have seen, the lack of neat correlation between one's biological lifespan and one's place in an inheritance scheme has been a feature of many of Shakespeare's plays. In the *Henry VI* plays and *Richard II* the father has perished too soon, leaving his immature successor without protection; in the *Henry IV* plays, on the other hand, an already-adult heir apparent seems to have nothing to do until his father dies. Prince Hal's enforced idleness ostensibly licenses bad behavior, but it also becomes a gift of "between-time" or "before-time" in which Hal does not yet need to perform as monarch. *King Lear* revisits this problem from the perspective of the elderly ruler rather than the perspective of those who will succeed him; in a sense, Lear, who wants to "shake all cares and business from our age" (1.1.37), tries to grasp near the end of his life the opportunity Prince Hal is afforded in his youth. Like Prince Hal, Lear can therefore be construed as a kind of prodigal. Goneril deplores the behavior of his retainers—"Men so disordered, so deboshed and bold | That this our court, infected with their manners | Shows like a riotous inn" (1.4.217–19). Regan claims that his companions aim only at Lear's ruin, "th'expense and waste of his revenues" (2.1.101). The retainers, in other words, are characterized as the prodigal's companions, partying with the "friend" they are victimizing. The point is not that the daughters' hostile descriptions are necessarily accurate or justified but that the imputation of prodigality seems, with Lear as with Hal, inevitably to follow upon the disruption of the "normal" inheritance expectations.

Yet is Lear's behavior really heedless, and is his expectation that his children will care for him in fact unreasonable? Richard Strier, who views Lear's self-divestiture as initially a reasonable plan of action, points to the example of the Holy Roman Emperor, Charles V.[16] In 1557, Charles resigned his office and territories to his son, Philip, and thereafter, as respected head of his family, lived in tranquil retirement in a modest house annexed to a monastery. Why doesn't Lear enjoy a similar outcome? Lear's pre-Christian Britain, of course, is devoid of monasteries, and the care of the old therefore falls to younger family members. Goneril and Regan perceive their father's weakness, as Edmund does his, but each thinks that senescence gives them an excuse to exploit rather than care for their parent. "Sons at perfect age, and fathers declining, the father should be as ward to the son, and the son manage his revenue," Edmund pretends Edgar has opined (1.2.68–70); when Goneril remarks that "old fools are babes again" (1.3.19), she imagines herself punishing rather than nurturing the wayward child. Since the frail elderly can no longer maintain their authority by intellectual superiority or physical force, any respect they receive from their children is an acknowledgement, by the children, that their own current thriving is predicated upon the generosity of those who have come before them. The loving provision of care issues from the memory of past benefits even if the flow of advantages does not continue into the present. Moreover, the children might also recognize that a system that honors parents will ultimately benefit themselves as they age in turn. In other words, the "duty" of adult children is a function of the way memory both keeps the past alive in the present and permits predictions about the future, encouraging an awareness of how individuals fit within a temporal sequence. Thus Lear prays that the goddess Nature revenge Goneril's ingratitude upon her in the next generation:

> If she must teem,
> Create her child of spleen, that it may live
> And be a thwart, disnatured torment to her!
> Let it stamp wrinkles in her brow of youth;
> With cadent tears fret channels in her cheeks,
> Turn all her mother's pains and benefits
> To laughter and contempt.

(1.4.259–64)

But his threats and curses fall on deaf ears because Goneril cares no more about the future than about the past. As Edwin Muir remarks, Goneril, Regan, and Edmund

see [things] in a continuous present divested of all associations, denuded of memory and the depth which memory gives to life... Having no memory, they have no responsibility.[17]

Rather like the unstrained mercy or the honorable liberality of *The Merchant of Venice*, gratitude cannot, apparently, be enjoined by force of positive law but only by the internalized dictates of duty, honor, and filial affection: dictates recognized by some but not by all of the characters in the play.

In its extra- or super-legal character, gratitude toward parents resembles, and in *King Lear* is eventually conflated with, the responsibility of the affluent to care for the indigent and the insane, who likewise have a legally unenforceable claim upon the resources of those who, in the present moment, happen to be more fortunate. Margot Heinemann writes:

> The heart of the political interest [in *Lear*] is not in the division of the kingdom or the issue of unification with Scotland, though there may well be allusions to this.... The causes of disaster lie deeper than that. The central focus is on the horror of a society divided between extremes of rich and poor, greed and starvation, the powerful and the powerless, robes and rags, and the impossibility of real justice and security in such a world.[18]

As in *2 Henry VI*, in other words, the problems of distributive justice are apparently both distinct from, and more profound than, problems of entitlement. Yet it is also important that in *Lear*, the suffering poor are not a different group from the entitled rich, but the same persons at different points in time. Poor Tom, who "swallows the old rat and the ditch-dog, drinks the green mantle of the standing-pool, who is whipped from tithing to tithing and stock punished, and imprisoned" can nonetheless recall a time in which he "had three suits to his back, six shirts to his body, horse to ride, and weapon to wear" (3.4.121–5). Moreover, of course, poor Tom is really Edgar, who is heir to a dukedom. His, and the other main characters', radical reversals of fortune differentiate *Lear* from *2 Henry VI*. In the early play, the obviousness of Cade's imposter status has the effect of segregating the problems of entitlement and the problems of distributive justice in different parts of the play. *2 Henry VI* largely confines the first issue to the "high plot" and the second to the "low plot." In *Lear*, however, the distinction between these two issues, and these two domains, eventually collapses.

What are the effects of this collapse? On the one hand, as de Grazia shrewdly observes, property is, in *Lear*, both a defining line between humans and beasts, and something extra, "a dispensable item that is all the same constitutive":[19]

> Our basest beggars
> Are in the poorest things superfluous.
> Allow not nature more than nature needs,
> Man's life is cheap as beast's.
>
> (2.4.259–62)

De Grazia's argument recalls Derrida's analysis of the "supplement" which is both an add-on and a vital part of that to which it is added.[20] In *Lear*, the property that in times of prosperity and stability seems constitutive of identity is in fact patently appliqué, even in the case of the basest beggars. However, then, because it is so easily detachable, it can seem at the same time *not* constitutive. Gazing on the nearly naked Poor Tom—significantly, as the Fool notes, he does possess a single blanket—Lear is overwhelmed with the conviction that the "real" person can emerge only when the appliqué is removed.

> Is man no more than this? Consider him well. Thou owest the worm no silk, the beast no hide, the sheep no wool, the cat no perfume.... Thou art the thing itself, unaccommodated man is no more but such a poor, bare, forked animal as thou art. Off, off, you lendings! Come unbutton here.
> *Tearing off his clothes.*
>
> (3.4.95–101)

For de Grazia, this attempt to delaminate the person from his belongings is absurd, and it is, of course, marked as "mad" in the play. And yet Shakespeare's fools and madmen are conduits to truth, and Lear seems as insightful here as he is crazy. He leans simultaneously on both contradictory wings of the paradoxical relation between being and having which we have seen manifested so often, in less extreme forms, in a considerable swath of Shakespeare's plays.

In 2 *Henry VI* the mutability of fortune produces an endless cycle of retributive violence as the newly vagabond struggle to reclaim what they believe to be their entitlements from the "pirates" who have appropriated them. In *Lear*, by contrast, the experience of immiseration, crushing the fortunate man's fantasy of exemption from suffering, encourages an empathetic impulse to distribute resources widely. Subjected to the storm on the heath, Lear cries:

> Poor, naked wretches, wheresoe'er you are,
> That bide the pelting of this pitiless storm,
> How shall your houseless heads and unfed sides,
> Your looped and windowed raggedness, defend you
> From seasons such as these? O, I have ta'en
> Too little care of this! Take physic, pomp,
> Expose thyself to feel what wretches feel,
> That thou may shake the superflux to them
> And show the heavens more just.

> > (3.4.29–37)

Heretofore Lear's privilege and power has literally insulated him from "what wretches feel"; now that he shares their "looped and windowed raggedness," he belatedly understands that wealth should be spread to alleviate misery. Gloucester echoes this sentiment:

> Let the superfluous and lust-dieted man
> That slaves your ordinance, that will not see
> Because he doth not feel, feel your power quickly;
> So distribution should undo excess,
> And each man have enough.

> > (4.1.67–71)

If, on the one hand, as de Grazia argues, property, "the superflux," is defined as that that which makes us human, it is apparently only by shaking off the "superflux" and becoming aware of the "unaccommodated" naked condition, which we all share, that we become humane. What Lear and Gloucester envisage is not a social revolution or institutional innovation that would eliminate privation, but simply a more lavish almsgiving by the rich, who, motivated by fellow-feeling, voluntarily bestow their "superflux" upon those who need it.

Unfortunately, in the absence of fellow-feeling this generous distribution will fail to occur. Like Goneril, incapable of understanding that she, like Lear, will one day be old, the "lust-dieted man" fails to see any connection between the vagabond and himself. "O, I have ta'en | Too little care of this!" admits Lear. Surrounded by plenty, he had little reason to empathize with the radically deprived; now that he himself is exposed to what wretches feel, he lacks the resources to remedy their plight. Moreover the craziest and dirtiest of beggars, who therefore most need succor, are those least likely to elicit an empathetic response: "Who gives anything to poor Tom?" (3.4.51). Whereas in *2 Henry VI* the problem of distribution troubles without displacing the problem of entitlement, in *Lear* entitlement seems to hinder appropriate distribution. In consequence, as the play proceeds, abstract questions of entitlement ultimately seem less critical than the relief that a creature with resources owes to one who has nothing:

> Had you not been their father, these white flakes
> Had challenged pity of them.
> ...
>   Mine enemy's dog,
> Though he had bit me, should have stood that night
> Against my fire.
>
> (4.7.30–8)

For Cordelia, the ethical requirements of distributive justice perhaps originate in, but do not require, a personal relationship between the reliever and the relieved. Even the enemy's dog may deserve succor.

Another important lesson of immiseration is that detachment from property transforms perceived value. It is easy for Lear to argue, before he is actually in need, that "Our basest beggars | Are in the poorest things superfluous" (2.4.259–60). At this point in the play, a reduction of one hundred retainers to a mere fifty seems utterly intolerable. Soon, however, Lear's own unhoused condition clarifies to him how drastically possessions can be pruned away, and how little can suffice to sustain life—effectively, in other words, re-defining what counts as "necessary" and what as "superfluous." The middle acts of *Lear* take place not in the fertile parts of the kingdom over which human beings aspire to extend their sway—its "cham-paigns riched" and "wide-skirted meads"—but in wild spaces where property rights are uncertain or are not worth asserting—the barren, storm-swept heath; the cliffs by the sea from which poor men peril-ously pluck sampire; the beach, which, as Bradin Cormack has re-cently reminded us, constituted a domain in which private titles did not prevail.[21] And yet in these marginal, inhospitable areas the dif-ference between want and need seems to emerge strongly, just as the "true" body of the man, poor, bare, and forked, emerges from his "lendings" when his clothing is stripped away. "The art of our ne-cessities is strange | And can make vile things precious" (3.2.70). A hovel can keep the rain at bay as well as a palace. Flowering weeds can be fashioned into a king's crown. The dislocations of value in the middle acts of *Lear* register as a form of insanity, but also as a form of wisdom, just as the itineracy of the vagabond can figure simultaneously as affliction and as liberation.

In this radically disrupted universe, in which vile things are pre-cious and previously desirable things seem worthless or dispensable, how is one to distinguish between what is necessary and what is "superfluous"? How does one decide what and how to retain and what and how to relinquish? How can one know when "each man has enough" when what counts as "enough" seems so labile and so situation-dependent? What do the entitled owe to those without title to anything? In *2 Henry VI* the middle term, as represented by Iden's modest, unambitious prosperity, offers an alternative to the rapa-cious rootlessness at the cossetted top and the deprived bottom of the social hierarchy. Other than brief glimpses of Cornwall's serv-ants and Gloucester's tenants, *Lear* offers no such alternative. One is either a landed aristocrat, living in a palace and waited upon by troops of retainers, or one "abjure[s] all roofs" (2.4.203), and sur-vives by feeding on wall-newts and dog carcasses.

The disturbance in valuation produced by *Lear*'s wrenching al-terations of status in turn conditions our response to the end of the play. Near the close of *Lear*, Edgar vindicates his title and property in single combat with Edmund, who has stolen it from him. His victory recalls the final scene of *1 Henry IV,* in which the true heir, Prince Hal, similarly triumphs over the rival who would displace him. This is also the fantasy York nurses in the *Henry VI* plays: that the supposed "vagabond" will return and, in a melodramatic act of justified violence, reveal his true identity and finally ascend to his deserved social place. Indeed, the vision of justified vengeance exacted by the unrecognized exile in his homecoming is so gratifying that it has driven literary endings since *The Odyssey.* In *Lear,* the contestants themselves comment upon its apparent inevitability. "The gods are just," opines Edgar after he trounces Edmund, and Edmund agrees: "Thou hast spoken right. 'Tis true, | The wheel has come full circle" (5.3.169, 172–3).

In *Lear,* however, the problem is of course that this climax is a false one. In fact, the stately ritual of the trial by combat, followed by Edgar's exposition of his sufferings, followed by the news of the deaths of the evil sisters—"this judgment of the heavens" (5.3.230)—all only divert attention from a more important concern. "Great thing of us forgot!" exclaims Albany (5.3.235): overly preoccupied with due process in his role as judge, and entranced by Edgar's melodramatic tale, he has permitted the plight of Lear and Cordelia simply to slip his mind. And their plight has likewise slipped the audience's mind as well—as if the pleasures of the familiar and neatly satisfying "literary" ending are not only distracting but positively dangerous, giving Edmund's henchman time to execute his purpose. This irony unavoidably troubles whatever satisfaction we derive from seeing that, as Margreta de Grazia notes, "the land seized from Edgar returns to him."[22] After the harrowing entrance of the howling "Lear, with Cordelia dead in his arms," who really cares that Edgar is now Duke of Gloucester? In fact, the restoration of Edgar's entitlement is part of a comprehensively disrupted recognition scene, in which the expected revelations occur but fail to register properly. Kent presents himself to Lear hoping for his king's gratitude for his loyal service, but Lear is too far gone to understand what his presence means. "The tragedy has outstripped Kent's scenario," as Michael Goldman asserts, and likewise Albany's "effort to play the role of the conventional leader who mops up capably and efficiently at the end of a tragedy...too is a promised end that has to be scrapped."[23]

At the end of the play, after the king's own death, the royal family of Britain is completely extinct. To whom does the kingdom now rightly belong? This is exactly the sort of ambiguous situation that has, again and again, produced the fierce strife of Shakespeare's earlier history plays. But here, Albany first demurs, resigning in favor of Kent and Edgar, and then Kent too declines to share the throne. By the end of the play, then, the "deserving" Edgar is not merely Duke of Gloucester, but, apparently, King of Britain. But it is a position that nobody seems to want. The apocalyptic language of the conclusion—"KENT Is this the promised end? EDGAR Or image of that horror?" (5.3.262–3)—suggests the extent to which the traumas of the play have made inheritance impossible. And it is impossible not only, or at least not primarily, because the royal family has been destroyed, but because the radical devaluation of what property might mean has emptied ambition of its motive by making it seem pointless. Who would want to rule Britain, and why? Edgar's last lines—"We that are young | Shall never see so much, nor live so long" (5.3.324–5)—suggest that nobody can or will step into the shoes of the ancestor. While in most of Shakespeare's plays, the theme of continual generational renewal underlies even the most disrupted property transfers, in *Lear* the very desirability of property, and the importance of asserting title to it, itself is at last emptied out.

After the devastations of *Lear*'s ending, it is hard likewise to end my own book; I feel myself somewhat in the embarrassed position of Edgar, obliged to say something stirring but at a loss as to what that might be. The simple conclusion about being and having in Shakespeare is that there is no simple conclusion. Reductive models of the way property and persons interact in Shakespeare's plays, and most likely in early modern life more generally, are seductive but misleading, even sentimental, just as Edgar's retrieval of his inheritance finally seems to be. Shakespeare inherits a religious and philosophical tradition of thinking about people and things that is, at its base, profoundly conflicted and contradictory. He lives in a society that distinguishes emphatically and in sophisticated ways between landed and chattel property, between the entitlements of daughters and the entitlements of sons, between what one owes to kin and what one owes to friends. Far from ignoring or glossing over those difficulties, Shakespeare broods intensely if intermittently upon them, making them extraordinarily productive but even less resolved.

Notes

1 A. L. Beier, *Masterless Men: The Vagrancy Problem in England 1560–1640* (New York: Methuen, 1985), pp. xxii, 18.

2 Beier, p. 70.

3 Francis Bacon, "Of Nobility," *The Essayes or Counsels, Civill and Morall,* ed. Michael Kiernan (Oxford: Clarendon Press, 1985), p. 42.

4 A W. B. Simpson, *A History of the Land Law*, second edition (Oxford: Clarendon Press, 1986), p. 150.

5 Ronald Knowles, "'The Farce of History': Miracle, Combat, and Rebellion in *2 Henry VI*" *Yearbook of English Studies* 21 (1991): 168–86 (185–6).

6 Jean Howard, "Introduction to *The First Part of the Contention*," in *The Norton Shakespeare*, second edition, ed. Stephen Greenblatt, Walter Cohen, Jean Howard, and Katharine Eisaman Maus (New York: W. W. Norton, 2008), pp. 203–90 (p. 235).

7 Stephen Greenblatt, "Murdering Peasants: Status, Genre, and the Representation of Rebellion," *Representations* 1 (1983): 1–29; Richard Helgerson, *Forms of Nationhood: The Elizabethan Writing of England* (Chicago, IL: Chicago University Press, 1992), pp. 195–245; Annabel Patterson, *Shakespeare and the Popular Voice* (Oxford: Basil Blackwell, 1989), pp. 32–51; Thomas Cartelli, "Jack Cade in the Garden: Class Consciousness and Class Conflict in *2 Henry VI*," in Richard Burt and John Michael Archer, eds., *Enclosure Acts: Sexuality, Property, and Culture in Early Modern England* (Ithaca, NY: Cornell University Press, 1994), pp. 48–64.

8 Helgerson, *Forms of Nationhood*, p. 206.

9 Richard Strier, *Resistant Structures: Particularity, Radicalism, and Renaissance Texts* (Berkeley, CA: University of California Press, 1995), p. 178.

10 Lynda E. Boose, "The Father and the Bride in Shakespeare," *PMLA* 97 (1982): 325–47 (332–5).

11 Stanley Cavell, "The Avoidance of Love: A Reading of *King Lear*," in *Disowning Knowledge in Six Plays of Shakespeare* (Cambridge: Cambridge University Press, 1987), pp. 39–124.

12 Margreta de Grazia, "The Ideology of Superfluous Things: *King Lear* as Period Piece," in Margreta de Grazia, Maureen Quilligan, and Peter Stallybrass, eds., *Subject and Object in Renaissance Culture* (Cambridge: Cambridge University Press, 1996), pp. 17–42 (p. 22).

13 de Grazia, p. 26.

14 Holinshed, Raphael, *Chronicles of England, Scotland, and Ireland* (London: J. Johnson, 1808) reprinted with an introduction by Vernon F. Snow (New York: AMS Press 1976), i, p. 447.

15 Cavell, p. 65.
16 Strier, *Resistant Structures*, p. 180.
17 Edwin Muir, *The Politics of King Lear* (New York: Haskell House, 1947), p. 17.
18 Margot Heinemann, "Demystifying the Mystery of State: *King Lear* and the World Upside Down," *Shakespeare Survey* 44 (1992): 75–83.
19 de Grazia, p. 22.
20 Jacques Derrida, *Of Grammatology*, trans. Gayatri Spivack (Baltimore, MD: Johns Hopkins University Press, 1997), pp. 141–64.
21 Bradin Cormack, *A Power to Do Justice: Jurisdiction, English Literature, and the Rise of Common Law, 1509–1625* (Chicago, IL: University of Chicago Press, 2007), pp. 227–90.
22 de Grazia, p. 25.
23 Michael Goldman, *Shakespeare and the Energies of Drama* (Princeton, NJ: Princeton University Press, 1972), pp. 106–7.

Bibliography

Ackerman, Bruce A., *Private Property and the Constitution* (New Haven, CT: Yale University Press, 1977).

Adelman, Janet, *Blood Relations: Christian and Jew in the Merchant of Venice* (Chicago, IL: University of Chicago Press, 2008).

Alexander, Gregory S., and Eduardo M. Penalver, eds., *Property and Community* (Oxford: Oxford University Press, 2010).

Aristotle, *The Basic Works*, ed. Richard McKeon (New York: Random House, 1941).

Auden, W. H., *The Dyer's Hand and Other Essays* (New York: Random House, 1962).

Bacon, Francis, *The Essays or Counsels, Civill and Morall*, ed. Michael Kiernan (Oxford: Clarendon Press, 1985).

Barber, C. L., *Shakespeare's Festive Comedy: A Study of Dramatic Form and Its Relation to Social Custom* (Princeton, NJ: Princeton University Press, 1959).

Becker, Lawrence C., *Property Rights—Philosophic Foundations* (London: Routledge, 1977).

Beier, A. L., *Masterless Men: The Vagrancy Problem in England 1560–1640* (New York: Methuen, 1985).

Bentham, Jeremy, *The Theory of Legislation*, trans. and ed. Charles Milner Atkinson from the French of Etienne Dumont (Oxford: Oxford University Press, 1914).

Berger, Harry, "Marriage and Mercifixion in *The Merchant of Venice*," *Shakespeare Quarterly* 32 (1981): 155–62.

Blackstone, Sir William, *Commentaries on the Laws of England*, ii: Of the Rights of Things (London: T. Cadell and W. Davies, 1809).

Boose, Lynda E., "The Father and the Bride in Shakespeare," *PMLA* 97 (1982): 325–47.

Bray, Alan, *Homosexuality in Renaissance England* (London: Gay Men's Press, 1982).

——, *The Friend* (Chicago, IL: University of Chicago Press, 2003).

Bright, Susan, and John Dewar, eds., *Land Law: Themes and Perspectives* (Oxford: Oxford University Press, 1998).

Bruster, Douglas, *Shakespeare and the Question of Culture* (New York: Palgrave Macmillan, 2003).

Cartelli, Thomas, "Jack Cade in the Garden: Class Consciousness and Class Conflict in *2 Henry VI*," in Richard Burt and John Michael Archer, eds., *Enclosure Acts: Sexuality, Property, and Culture in Early Modern England* (Ithaca, NY: Cornell University Press, 1994), pp. 48–64.

Cavell, Stanley, *Disowning Knowledge in Six Plays of Shakespeare* (Cambridge: Cambridge University Press, 1987).

Clarkson, L. A., *The Pre-Industrial Economy in England 1500–1750* (London: Batsford, 1971).

Cohen, Morris, "Property and Sovereignty," *Cornell Law Quarterly* 13 (1927): 8–30.

Cooper, J. P., *Land, Men, and Beliefs: Studies in Early Modern History* (London: Hambledon Press, 1983).

Cormack, Bradin, *A Power to Do Justice: Jurisdiction, English Literature, and the Rise of Common Law, 1509–1625* (Chicago, IL: University of Chicago Press, 2007).

Danson, Lawrence, *The Harmonies of the Merchant of Venice* (New Haven, CT: Yale University Press, 1978).

de Grazia, Margreta, "The Ideology of Superfluous Things: *King Lear* as Period Piece," in Margreta de Grazia, Maureen Quilligan, and Peter Stallybrass, eds., *Subject and Object in Renaissance Culture* (Cambridge: Cambridge University Press, 1996), pp. 17–42.

——*Hamlet Without Hamlet* (Cambridge: Cambridge University Press, 2007).

——, Maureen Quilligan, and Peter Stallybrass, eds., *Subject and Object in Renaissance Culture* (Cambridge: Cambridge University Press, 1996).

Derrida, Jacques, *Of Grammatology*, trans. Gayatri Spivack (Baltimore, MD: Johns Hopkins University Press, 1997).

Engle, Lars, *Shakespearean Pragmatism: Market of His Time* (Chicago, IL: University of Chicago Press, 1993).

Erickson, Amy Louise, *Women and Property in Early Modern England* (London: Routledge, 1993).

Feerick, Jean, " 'Divided by soyle': Plantation and Degeneracy in *The Tempest* and *The Sea Voyage*," *Renaissance Drama* 35 (2006): 27–54.

Findlay, Heather, "Renaissance Pederasty and Pedagogy: the 'Case' of Shakespeare's Falstaff," *Yale Journal of Criticism* 3 (1989): 229–38.

Forker, Charles R., ed., *Richard II*, Shakespeare: The Critical Tradition (London: Athlone Press, 1998).

Fumerton, Patricia, and Simon Hunt, eds., *Renaissance Culture and the Everyday* (Philadelphia, PA: University of Pennsylvania Press, 1999).

Goldberg, Jonathan, *Sodometries: Renaissance Texts, Modern Sexualities* (Stanford, CA: Stanford University Press, 1992).

Goldman, Michael, *Shakespeare and the Energies of Drama* (Princeton, NJ: Princeton University Press, 1972).

Goody, Jack, Joan Thirsk, and E.P. Thompson, eds., *Family and Inheritance in Western Europe 1200–1800* (Cambridge: Cambridge University Press, 1978).

Granville-Barker, Harley, *Prefaces to Shakespeare* (London: Sidgwick and Jackson, 1935).

Greenblatt, Stephen, "Murdering Peasants: Status, Genre, and the Representation of Rebellion," *Representations* 1 (1983): 1–29.

Gurlyand, Ilia, "Reminiscences of A. P. Chekhov," *Teatr i iskusstvo* (11 July 1904).

Habakkuk, John, *Marriage, Debt, and the Estates System: English Landownership 1650–1950* (Oxford: Clarendon Press, 1994).

Hamilton, Donna, "The State of Law in *Richard II*," *Shakespeare Quarterly* 34 (1983): 5–17.

Harris, Jonathan Gil, *Untimely Matter in the Time of Shakespeare* (Philadelphia, PA: University of Pennsylvania Press, 2009).

——, and Natasha Korda, eds., *Staged Properties in Early Modern English Drama* (Cambridge: Cambridge University Press, 2002).

Harris, J. W., *Property and Justice* (Oxford: Clarendon Press, 1996).

Harrison, William, *A Description of England*, ed. Georges Edelen (Ithaca, NY: Cornell University Press, 1968).

Hawkes, David, "Materialism and Reification in Renaissance Studies," *Journal of Early Modern Cultural Studies* 4 (2004): 114–29.

Heinemann, Margot, "Demystifying the Mystery of State: *King Lear* and the World Upside Down," *Shakespeare Survey* 44 (1992): 75–83.

Helgerson, Richard, *The Elizabethan Prodigals* (Berkeley, CA: University of California Press, 1976).

——, *Forms of Nationhood: The Elizabethan Writing of England* (Chicago, IL: Chicago University Press, 1992).

Henriques, H. S. Q., *The Jews and English Law* (London: J. Jacobs, 1908).

Holinshed, Raphael, *Chronicles of England, Scotland, and Ireland* (London: J. Johnson, 1808), reprinted with an introduction by Vernon F. Snow (New York: AMS Press, 1976).

Holmes, Oliver Wendell, "The Path of the Law," *Harvard Law Review* 10 (1897): 457–78.

Hutson, Lorna, *The Usurer's Daughter* (London: Routledge, 1994).

Jones, Ann Rosalind, and Peter Stallybrass, *Renaissance Clothing and the Materials of Memory* (Cambridge: Cambridge University Press, 2000).

Kantorowicz, Ernst, *The King's Two Bodies: A Study in Medieval Political Theology* (Princeton, NJ: Princeton University Press, 1957).

Kerridge, Eric, *Agrarian Problems in the Sixteenth Century and After* (New York: Barnes and Noble, 1969).

Kneidel, Gregory, "Coscus, Queen Elizabeth, and Law in John Donne's *Satyre II*," *Renaissance Quarterly* 61 (2009): 92–121.

Knowles, Robert, "'The Farce of History': Miracle, Combat, and Rebellion in *2 Henry VI*," *Yearbook of English Studies* 21 (1991): 168–86.

Korda, Natasha, *Shakespeare's Domestic Economies: Gender and Property in Early Modern England* (Philadelphia, PA: University of Pennsylvania Press, 2002).

Landreth, David, *The Face of Mammon: The Matter of Money in English Renaissance Literature* (Oxford: Oxford University Press, 2012).

Lewalski, Barbara, "Biblical Allusion and Allegory in *The Merchant of Venice*," *Shakespeare Quarterly* 13 (1962): 327–43.

McAlindon, T. A., *Shakespeare's Tudor History: A Study of Henry IV, parts 1 and 2* (Aldershot: Ashgate, 2001).

Macpherson, C. B., ed., *Property: Mainstream and Critical Traditions* (Toronto: University of Toronto Press, 1978).

Maus, Katharine, "Satiric and Ideal Economies in the Jonsonian Imagination," *English Literary Renaissance* 19 (1989): 42–64.

Muir, Edwin, *The Politics of King Lear* (New York: Haskell House, 1947).

Muldrew, Craig, *The Economy of Obligation: The Culture of Credit and Social Relations in Early Modern England* (London: Palgrave Macmillan, 1998).

Munzer, Steven, *A Theory of Property* (Cambridge: Cambridge University Press, 1990).

Nedelsky, Jennifer, *Private Property and the Limits of American Constitutionalism: The Madisonian Framework and Its Legacy* (Chicago, IL: University of Chicago Press, 1990).

Newman, Karen, "Portia's Ring: Unruly Women and the Structure of Exchange in *The Merchant of Venice*," *Shakespeare Quarterly* 38 (1987): 19–33.

Ornstein, Robert, *A Kingdom for A Stage: The Achievement of Shakespeare's History Plays* (Cambridge, MA: Harvard University Press, 1972).

Patterson, Annabel, *Shakespeare and the Popular Voice* (Oxford: Basil Blackwell, 1989).

Penner, J. E., *The Idea of Property in Law* (Oxford: Clarendon Press, 1997).

Plato, *Complete Works*, ed. John M. Cooper (Indianapolis, IN: Hackett, 1997).

Plowden, Edmund, Sharington v. Strotton (1566), in *The Commentaries or Reports…Containing Divers Cases upon Matters of Law* (London: S. Brooke, 1816), pp. 298–309.

Popham, Sir John, *Reports and Cases*, second edition (London: John Place, 1682)

Purdy, Jedediah, *The Meaning of Property: Freedom, Community, and the Legal Imagination* (New Haven, CT: Yale University Press, 2010).

Radin, Margaret, *Reinterpreting Property* (Chicago, IL: University of Chicago Press, 1993).

Rose, Carol, *Property and Persuasion: Essays on the History, Theory, and Rhetoric of Ownership* (Boulder, CO: Westview Press, 1994).

Rubinstein, E., "*1 Henry IV*: The Metaphor of Liability," *Studies in English Literature, 1500–1900* 10:2 (1970): 287–95.

Schweiker, William, and Charles Mathewes, eds., *Having: Property and Possession in Religious and Social Life* (Grand Rapids, MI: Eerdmans, 2004).

Scott, William O., "Landholding, Leasing, and Inheritance in *Richard II*" *Studies in English Literature 1500–1900* 42:2 (2002): 275–92.

Shakespeare, William, *The Norton Shakespeare*, second edition, ed. Stephen Greenblatt, Walter Cohen, Jean Howard, and Katharine Eisaman Maus (New York: W. W. Norton, 2008).

Shannon, Laurie, *Sovereign Amity: Figures of Friendship in Shakespearean Contexts* (Chicago, IL: University of Chicago Press, 2002).

——, "Likenings: Rhetorical Husbandries and Portia's 'True Conceit' of Friendship," *Renaissance Drama* New Series 31 (2002): 3–26.

Sharp, Ronald A., "Gift Exchange and the Economies of Spirit in *The Merchant of Venice*," *Modern Philology* 83 (1986): 250–65.

Shell, Mark, "The Wether and the Ewe: Verbal Usury in *The Merchant of Venice*," *Kenyon Review* 1:4 (1979): 65–72.

Simpson, A. W. B., *A History of the Land Law*, second edition (Oxford: Clarendon Press, 1986).

Singer, Joseph William, *Entitlement: The Paradoxes of Property* (New Haven, CT: Yale University Press, 2000).

Sinfield, Alan, "How to Read *The Merchant of Venice* Without Being Heterosexist," in Terence Hawkes, ed., *Alternative Shakespeares*, ii (London: Routledge, 1996), pp. 122–39.

Sofer, Andrew, *The Stage Life of Props* (Ann Arbor, MI: University of Michigan Press, 2004).

Slack, Paul, *Poverty and Policy in Tudor and Stuart England* (New York: Longman, 1988).

Spring, Eileen, *Law, Land, and Family: Aristocratic Inheritance in England, 1300–1800* (Chapel Hill, NC: University of North Carolina Press, 1993).

Stallybrass, Peter, "The Value of Culture and the Disavowal of Things," in Henry S. Turner, ed., *The Culture of Capital: Property, Cities, and Knowledge in Early Modern England* (New York: Routledge, 2002), pp. 275–92.

Stewart, Alan, *Shakespeare's Letters* (Oxford: Oxford University Press, 2008).

Stone, Lawrence, *Crisis of the Aristocracy, 1558–1641* (Oxford: Oxford University Press, 1965).

Stretton, Tim, *Women Waging Law in Elizabethan England* (Cambridge: Cambridge University Press, 1998).

Strier, Richard, *Resistant Structures: Particularity, Radicalism, and Renaissance Texts* (Berkeley, CA: University of California Press, 1995).

Thirsk, Joan, *Economic Policy and Projects: The Development of a Consumer Society in Early Modern England* (Oxford: Clarendon Press, 1978).

Turner, Henry S., "The Problem of the More-Than-One: Friendship, Calculation, and Political Association in *The Merchant of Venice*," *Shakespeare Quarterly* 57 (2006): 413–42.

——, ed., *The Culture of Capital: Property, Cities, and Knowledge in Early Modern England* (New York: Routledge, 2002).

Underkuffler, Laura, *The Idea of Property: Its Meaning and Power* (Oxford: Oxford University Press, 2003).

Waldron, Jeremy, *The Right to Private Property*. (Oxford: Clarendon Press, 1988).

Weiner, Annette B., *Inalienable Possessions: The Paradox of Keeping-While-Giving* (Berkeley, CA: University of California Press, 1992).

Wheater, Isabella, "Aristotelian Wealth and the Sea of Love: Shakespeare's Synthesis of Greek Philosophy and Roman Poetry in *The Merchant of Venice*," *Review of English Studies* New Series 43 (1992): 467–87 and 44 (1993): 16–36.

Whittle, Jane, "Leasehold Tenure in England c.1300-c.1600: Its Form and Incidence," in Bas J.P. van Bavel and Phillipp R. Schofield, eds., *The Development of Leasehold in Northwestern Europe, c.1200–1600* (Turnhout, Belgium: Brepols, 2008), pp. 139–54.

Wilson, Luke, "Drama and Marine Insurance in Shakespeare's London" in Constance Jordan and Karen Cunningham, eds., *The Law in Shakespeare* (London: Palgrave Macmillan, 2007), pp. 127–42.

Wootton, David, ed., *Divine Right and Democracy: An Anthology of Political Writing in Stuart England* (London: Hackett, 2003).

Wrightson, Keith, *Earthly Necessities: Economic Lives in Early Modern Britain* (New Haven, CT: Yale University Press, 2002).

Yates, Julian, *Error Misuse Failure: Object Lessons from the English Renaissance* (Minneapolis, MN: University of Minnesota Press, 2003).

Index